SHEPHERD'S NOTES

Shepherd's Notes Titles Available

SHEPHERD'S NOTES COMMENTARY SERIES

Old Testament

New Testament

SHEPHERD'S NOTES CHRISTIAN CLASSICS

SHEPHERD'S NOTES-BIBLE SUMMARY SERIES

SHEPHERD'S NOTES

When you need a guide through the Scriptures

Ezra/ Nehemiah

BROADMAN
& HOLMAN
PUBLISHERS

Nashville, Tennessee

Shepherd's Notes®—*Ezra and Nehemiah*
© 1999
by Broadman & Holman Publishers
Nashville, Tennessee
All rights reserved
Printed in the United States of America

0–8054–9194–5
Dewey Decimal Classification: 222.70
Subject Heading: BIBLE. O.T. EZRA
Library of Congress Card Catalog Number: 98–48093

Library of Congress Cataloging-in-Publication Data
Bergen, Martha, 1954-
Ezra & Nehemiah / Martha Bergen, editor [i.e. author].
     p. cm. — (Shepherd's notes)
    Includes bibliographical references.
    ISBN 0–8054–9194–5 (trade paper)
    1. Bible. O.T. Ezra—Study and teaching.   2. Bible. O.T. Nehemiah—Study
and teaching. I. Title. II. Title: Ezra and Nehemiah. III. Series
BS1355.5.B47   1999
222'.707—dc21   98–48093
                                                                    CIP

2 3 4 5 6 7   08 07 06 05 04

CONTENTS

FOREWORD

Dear Reader:

Shepherd's Notes are designed to give you a quick, step-by-step overview of every book of the Bible. They are not meant to be substitutes for the biblical text; rather, they are study guides intended to help you explore the wisdom of Scripture in personal or group study and to apply that wisdom successfully in your own life.

Shepherd's Notes guide you through the main themes of each book of the Bible and illuminate fascinating details through appropriate commentary and reference notes. Historical and cultural background information brings the Bible into sharper focus.

Six different icons, used throughout the series, call your attention to historical-cultural information, Old Testament and New Testament references, word pictures, unit summaries, and personal application for everyday life.

Whether you are a novice or a veteran at Bible study, I believe you will find *Shepherd's Notes* a resource that will take you to a new level in your mining and applying the riches of Scripture.

In Him,

David R. Shepherd
Editor-in-Chief

HOW TO USE THIS BOOK

DESIGNED FOR THE BUSY USER

Shepherd's Notes for Ezra and Nehemiah is designed to provide an easy-to-use tool for getting a quick handle on these significant Bible books' important features, and for gaining an understanding of their messages. Information available in more difficult-to-use reference works has been incorporated into the *Shepherd's Notes* format. This brings you the benefits of many advanced and expensive works packed into one small volume.

Shepherd's Notes are for laymen, pastors, teachers, small-group leaders and participants, as well as the classroom student. Enrich your personal study or quiet time. Shorten your class or small-group preparation time as you gain valuable insights into the truths of God's Word that you can pass along to your students or group members.

DESIGNED FOR QUICK ACCESS

Bible students with time constraints will especially appreciate the timesaving features built into the *Shepherd's Notes*. All features are intended to aid a quick and concise encounter with the heart of the messages of Ezra and Nehemiah.

Concise Commentary. Short sections provide quick "snapshots" of the themes of these books, highlighting important points and other information.

Outlined Text. Comprehensive outlines cover the entire text of Ezra and Nehemiah. This is a valuable feature for following each book's flow, allowing for a quick, easy way to locate a particular passage.

Shepherd's Notes. These summary statements or capsule thoughts appear at the close of every key section of the narratives. While functioning in part as a quick summary, they also deliver the essence of the message presented in the sections which they cover.

Icons. Various icons in the margin highlight recurring themes in the books of Ezra and Nehemiah, aiding in selective searching or tracing of those themes.

Sidebars and Charts. These specially selected features provide additional background information to your study or preparation. Charts offer a quick overview of important subjects. Sidebars include definitions as well as cultural, historical, and biblical insights.

Questions to Guide Your Study. These thought-provoking questions and discussion starters are designed to encourage interaction with the truth and principles of God's Word.

DESIGNED TO WORK FOR YOU

Personal Study. Using the *Shepherd's Notes* with a passage of Scripture can enlighten your study and take it to a new level. At your fingertips is information that would require searching several volumes to find. In addition, many points of application occur throughout the volume, contributing to personal growth.

Teaching. Outlines frame the text of Ezra and Nehemiah, providing a logical presentation of their messages. Capsule thoughts designated as "Shepherd's Notes" provide summary statements for presenting the essence of key points and events. Personal Application icons point out personal application of the messages of the books. Historical Context icons indicate where cultural and historical background information is supplied.

Group Study. *Shepherd's Notes* can be an excellent companion volume to use for gaining a quick but accurate understanding of the messages of Ezra and Nehemiah. Each group member can benefit from having his or her own copy. The *Notes* format accommodates the study of themes throughout Ezra and Nehemiah. Leaders may use its flexible features to prepare for group sessions or use them during group sessions. Questions to guide your study can spark discussion of Ezra and

Nehemiah's key points and truths to be discovered in these delightful books.

LIST OF MARGIN ICONS USED IN EZRA AND NEHEMIAH

 Shepherd's Notes. Placed at the end of each section, a capsule statement provides the reader with the essence of the message of that section.

 Historical Context. To indicate historical information—historical, biographical, cultural—and provide insight on the understanding or interpretation of a passage.

 Old Testament Reference. Used when the writer refers to Old Testament passages or when Old Testament passages illuminate a text.

 New Testament Reference. Used when the writer refers to New Testament passages that are either fulfilled prophecy, an antitype of an Old Testament type, or a New Testament text which in some other way illuminates the passages under discussion.

 Personal Application. Used when the text provides a personal or universal application of truth.

 Word Picture. Indicates that the meaning of a specific word or phrase is illustrated so as to shed light on it.

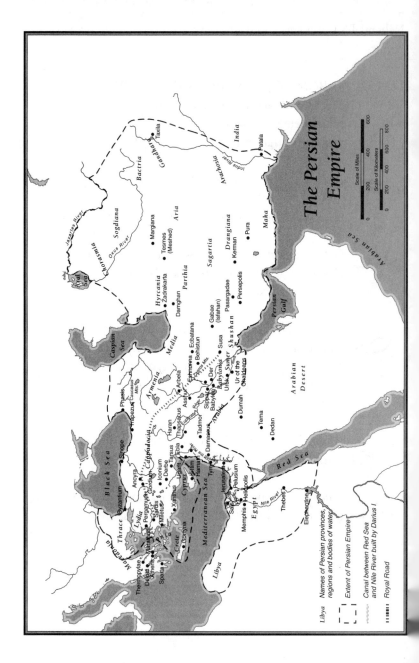

Taken from, Mervin Breneman, *Ezra, Nehemiah, Esther,* vol. 10, New American Commentary (Nashville, Tenn.: Broadman & Holman Publishers, 1993), p. 12.

INTRODUCTION

The books of Ezra and Nehemiah are believed to
have been originally separate books, although
they occur as one within the oldest Hebrew
manuscripts. Both fall within the division of the
Hebrew canon known as the Writings.
Nehemiah is the last of the Old Testament historical books. A close examination of both
books reveals several parallels or similarities:

- the return to Jerusalem to build something
  significant,
- opposition to the building project,
- confession of sin among the people, and
- the observance of a holy feast.

	EZRA	NEHEMIAH
BACKGROUND	Priestly family; scribe; teacher of the Law	Layman with administrative skills; cupbearer to king
DATE BOOK WRITTEN	440 B.C.	430 B.C.
PERSIAN KING	Cyrus; founder of Persian Empire	Artaxerxes
PURPOSE OF RETURN	Rebuild Temple	Rebuild city walls
DATE PROJECT COMPLETED	ca. 516 B.C.	52 days
ENEMIES	People of Samaria	Sanballat, Tobiah, and Geshem
SOCIAL CONCERNS/SINS	Marriage to foreigners	Wealthy Jews abuse poorer Jews; intermarriage; neglect of Sabbath and Temple duties
CELEBRATION FEAST	Passover	Tabernacles/Booths

The Greek translation of the Old Testament, known as the Septuagint (LXX), includes Ezra and Nehemiah as one book. Within the Latin Vulgate, Jerome referred to these as I Ezra and II Ezra. The Jewish historian Josephus, as well as the Jewish Talmud (commentary on oral law), mention the book of Ezra but not a separate book of Nehemiah.

The prophets spoke of this long before it ever came to be. Recorded in Jeremiah, for example, are the words, "I will bring Judah and Israel back from captivity and will rebuild them as they were before" (Jer. 33:7).

Three common dates for Nebuchadnezzar's deportation of the Jews into exile are 605 B.C. (Daniel among group); 597 B.C. (Ezekiel among group); and 586 B.C. (the majority of Jews).

PURPOSE

Both books show God's sovereignty and faithfulness in fulfilling His promise to the people of Israel that they would be restored to their homeland after having been exiled in Babylon.

Beginning with Abraham, God promised He would raise up a group of people to be His own to bring Him glory. God blessed the nation of Israel and used her to bless others. Ultimately this was fulfilled in the coming of the Messiah (Christ). Now, for more than fifty years God's people had been exiled in Babylon. Their sin against God had resulted in their being removed from their homeland.

In Ezra, God's people returned to rebuild the Temple; in Nehemiah, the purpose was to rebuild the wall around Jerusalem. A related purpose, particularly of the book of Ezra, was to serve as encouragement for the Jewish remnant to remain faithful to the worship of God, especially as it related to worship associated with the Temple.

The Temple and the wall were two important elements of Israel's identity—both nationally and spiritually—which relate to God's promise. Although in judgment God had "broken down his Temple as though it were . . . a garden" (Lam. 2:6, NLT) and had "determined to destroy the walls of Jerusalem" (Lam. 2:8, NLT), once again these would exist; and the nation would flourish and be strong. The wall would fortify the city and provide a means of defense and protection. And the Temple would serve as a means to unify the people, offset heathenism, and serve as a place for the worship of God. In all of this, Israel would be a testimony to God's sovereignty, dependability, and faithfulness.

AUTHORSHIP AND DATE

No claim is given in either book as to authorship. Ezra, however, is traditionally accepted as the author of the book which bears his name. Some scholars see both books as having been penned by the same person, with this person perhaps also having written 1 and 2 Chronicles. With portions of Nehemiah being written in the first person, it is reasonable to conclude that the man Nehemiah wrote this book. Since Ezra was a scribe, he might possibly have edited the book of Nehemiah. Thus, Ezra could have been involved somewhat in the structure and formation of both books.

The time period for the completion of both Ezra and Nehemiah is similar. While there may be variation among some biblical scholars as to dating, the approximate date of Ezra's composition ranges from 450 to 440 B.C. Nehemiah, on the other hand, was written approximately 430 B.C.

The setting for the opening of Ezra is during the first year of King Cyrus (Ezra 1:1). Cyrus was the founder of the Persian Empire. In 539 B.C., Cyrus conquered Babylon and so became ruler of the Jews who were in Babylon. He was sympathetic toward them and allowed them to return to Jerusalem. The book recounts the details of their return and their efforts to rebuild the Temple. Ezra concludes with the Israelites gathering in Jerusalem to confess their sin around the year 458 B.C.

Nehemiah, on the other hand, returned to Jerusalem for the purpose of rebuilding the city's walls during the year 445 B.C., the twentieth year of the reign of the Persian king Artaxerxes (Neh. 2:1). As the book concludes, the

Do you sometimes doubt God's faithfulness in your life? It is easy to forget His promises, especially if long periods of time pass before they are fulfilled. Israel had to wait at least fifty years after her captivity before returning to her homeland. That's more than half a lifetime. God is faithful, and His dependability is not measured by time. When He makes a promise, no matter how long He may take, He keeps it!

Ezra means "help." *Nehemiah* means "the Lord is compassionate."

Zerubbabel, the governor of Samaria, led the first return in 538 B.C. The second group, under Ezra, returned in 458 B.C. Nehemiah's return was in 445 B.C.

king is said to be in his thirty-second year (Neh. 13:6). Not all the Jews who returned to Jerusalem did so at the same time. This would account for the difference in Ezra's and Nehemiah's return. Ezra was not among the first group of Israelites who returned to Jerusalem to rebuild the Temple under the permission of King Cyrus. He did not return until a second group of Jews were allowed to do so in 458 B.C. By this time, King Artaxerxes was in power, having ruled for about seven years (Ezra 7:8).

LITERARY STYLE AND FORM

The literary style and form of the books of Ezra and Nehemiah differ. It appears, however, that both are organized around topics rather than chronology. One of the most prominent features within both books, though more distinctive of Ezra, is their use of lists. These lists include such things as the names of exiles who return (see, for example, Ezra 2 and Neh. 7); vessels used within the Temple; persons who help rebuild the wall; and various Temple personnel, i.e., priests, Levites, gatekeepers, and singers. It is interesting to note that 1 and 2 Chronicles also utilize lists. Prominent are listings of Levites and various other Temple personnel.

Another feature which characterizes both books is the inclusion of each man's memoirs. Interestingly, the memoirs are divided into roughly equal parts and interleaved (Ezra I [Ezra 7:1–10:4]; Neh. I [Neh. 1:1–7:73a]; Ezra II [Neh. 7:73b–10:39]; and Neh. II [Neh. 11:1–13:3]). Included in them are such things as the account of each man's arrival at Jerusalem, the problem of mixed marriages, the building of the wall, and the reading of the Law.

Unique to Ezra are seven documents or letters of official correspondence, each of which deals with some aspect of the reason and purpose for the Jews' return. With the exception of the first letter—which is written in Hebrew—each of these is in Aramaic, the "international language" of the Persian period. These Aramaic sections are found in 4:8–6:18 and 7:12–26.

Approximately one quarter of the book of Ezra was written in Aramaic. Some scholars explain this by suggesting that Ezra found these Aramaic documents or letters and, as a scribe, simply copied them using Aramaic insertions to connect them. Since Aramaic was the official language during this time period, perhaps it was not so unusual that Ezra used it.

THEOLOGY

When reading Ezra and Nehemiah, several theological considerations emerge. One such consideration is God's sovereignty. God had a plan for His people Israel. And while at first glance it seems that that plan failed miserably, a closer look reveals a God who indeed accomplished His purposes. God in His sovereignty used not only the likes of an Ezra and a Nehemiah but also pagan kings such as Cyrus (Ezra 1:2) and even enemies of the Jews such as Sanballat and Tobiah (Neh. 4:7–9, 14–15) to achieve His sovereign will.

A third consideration is God's unconditional love. Ultimately, it was His enduring, committed love for Israel that allowed the Jewish remnant to survive and return to their homeland. It was this love that enabled Him to forgive their sin. When Jeremiah spoke of the promise of Israel's restoration, he remembered God's unending love and declared, "Give thanks to the LORD Almighty, for . . . His faithful love endures forever" (Jer. 33:11, NLT). God's love did not depend upon Israel's actions; He loved her solely because He wanted to love her.

MEANING AND RELEVANCE FOR TODAY

While the events of Ezra and Nehemiah took place hundreds of years before the birth of

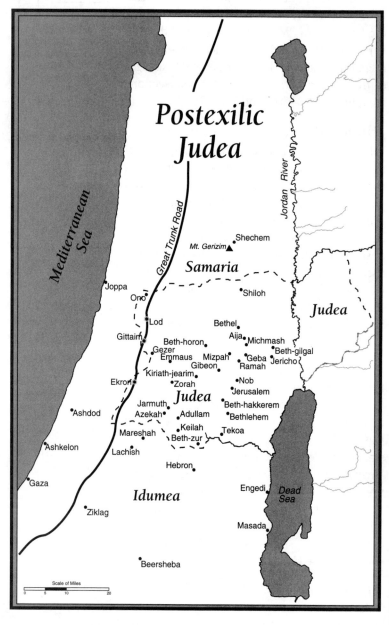

Taken from, Mervin Breneman, *Ezra, Nehemiah, Esther,* vol. 10, New American Commentary (Nashville, Tenn.: Broadman & Holman Publishers, 1993), p. 13.

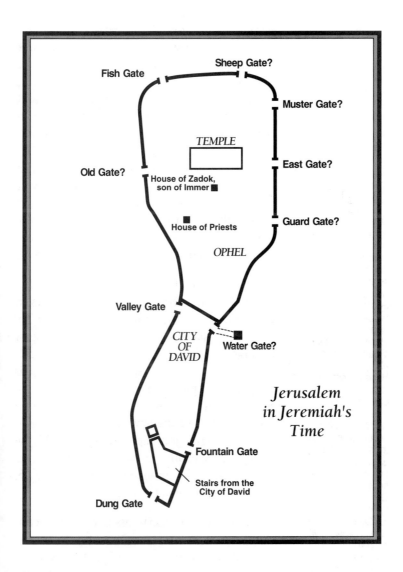

Taken from, Mervin Breneman, *Ezra, Nehemiah, Esther,* vol. 10, New American Commentary (Nashville, Tenn.: Broadman & Holman Publishers, 1993), p. 14.

Christ, principles from these books have relevant application for the Christian life today. Because God is sovereign, He has a distinct plan and purpose for every believer which ties into His perfect will. His supreme authority and power—extending over all creation and throughout all time—give evidence not only of His full control over people, things, and events but of His divine will and purpose for time and humanity as well. Questions regarding life's concerns, whether they be education, career, marriage, family, health, or finances, provide opportunities for the Christian to discover God's will and place confidence in His ability to work in all things for His good purpose (note Rom. 8:28; Phil. 1:6; 2:13).

As God pledged His faithfulness to Israel, so has He promised to be faithful to every believer. Christians may find Him trustworthy in all of life's circumstances, no matter how puzzling or troubling these may be. And when difficult tasks need to be done, God is there to help His people accomplish them, despite possible distraction and opposition. God's strength and presence enabled the Jews to rebuild the Temple and rebuild Jerusalem's city walls. In the same way He enables us to do what sometimes appears to be the impossible (see Matt. 19:26; 2 Cor. 12:9; and 1 John 4:4).

The Christian may also be assured of God's constant love—a love that can never be earned. His is a stubborn love because it is not based upon emotion; it is a deliberate choice. He loves "in spite of," not "because of." Christians today may feel that God cannot love them because of who they are or what they have done. God's love for sinful Israel reestablished her as a great nation. His love also enables Christians to be forgiven

Often it seems the world around us is falling apart. The very threads of our lives may ravel at the seams. We may wonder if God is aware of what's happening, much less able to do anything about it. Admittedly, circumstances are not always "good." However, difficult circumstances are often the means whereby we discover God's peace and dependability. In the midst of Judah's devastation, the prophet Jeremiah had hope as he recalled God's love and faithfulness (see Lam. 3:17–23). The truth is, God is dependable despite circumstances—whether they be good or bad. And for this reason, we may take heart and rejoice. God remains faithful and does what He says He will do!

and made anew (note John 3:16–17; Rom. 5:8; and 1 John 1:9).

QUESTIONS TO GUIDE YOUR STUDY

1. What are some features that Ezra and Nehemiah share?
2. What two elements were important in Israel's identity? Why were these important?
3. In which languages was Ezra written?
4. Which of God's attributes do we see most clearly in Ezra?

EZRA

THE FIRST RETURN FROM EXILE (1:1–11)

After approximately fifty years of Exile, the Jews were allowed to return to their homeland. They were not just a group who testified to the "survival of the fittest." They survived and were able to return solely because of God's love, grace, and mercy. He willfully spared them and brought them back for the purpose of His renown.

Fulfillment of Prophecy (1:1)

As the book of Ezra opens, the author indicates that Cyrus, the king of Persia, is in his first year of reign over the Babylonians/Jews. While such information is pertinent to his narrative, even more striking is the theological framework for his information. As the story unfolds, it is done so from the perspective of God's will and purpose for the Jews. Thus, what follows is not mere coincidence but the fulfillment of God's Word. And such is stated within the first verse of the book itself—a seemingly deliberate choice on the part of the writer. What happens is "in order to fulfill the word of the LORD" (NASB). And, as if there should be any doubt, reference is made specifically to the prophet Jeremiah as one whom God used to predict this very happening.

The author noted that it was God Himself who worked within the life of Cyrus to bring about his sympathies and kindnesses toward the Jewish people. "The LORD stirred up the spirit of Cyrus king of Persia" (NASB) and "moved the heart of Cyrus king of Persia" (NIV). This was no mere coincidence. God worked using a particu-

Cyrus (Hebrew "Koresh") was the founder of the great Medo-Persian Empire. Upon the death of his father in 559 B.C., he became king of the Persians and succeeded in conquering the Medes in 550 B.C. He was a rather shrewd politician who defeated the ancient kingdoms of Armenia, Cappadocia, Cilicia, and Lydia, as well as Greek colonies within Asia Minor (areas today known as Afghanistan, Iran, Iraq, Syria, and Turkey). Especially significant was his conquest and defeat of Babylon in 539 B.C. Having overtaken the Babylonian Empire, he now ruled Israel and Judah. His son Cambyses succeeded him in 530 B.C.

10

lar individual at a particular point in time to accomplish His particular purpose. Because of God's intervention, Cyrus issued a proclamation that was sent throughout all his kingdom allowing any Jew who wished to return to Jerusalem with the specific purpose of rebuilding the Temple. Not only was this edict orally proclaimed, but it was also put into writing.

■ *God caused Cyrus to issue a decree in fulfill-*
■ *ment of a prophetic promise.*

The Decree from Cyrus (1:2–4)

The edict itself gives evidence of Cyrus's acknowledgment of the Lord, the God of the Jews. While initially it sounds as if Cyrus may have feared and worshiped God, further study indicates that he was sympathetic toward the peoples under his subjection with respect to their gods and various religious customs and practices. His acknowledgment of the Lord and sympathies toward the Jews represented political savvy on his part. Thus, placating the gods of his peoples won him favor and helped to keep down revolt within his empire.

An examination of the biblical account of the edict reveals Cyrus's generosity toward the Jews. He did not pick a select few but allowed anyone to return who so desired. Not only that, but he also wished them God's blessing, "may his God be with him" (v. 3), and even made provisions for their resettlement in the land as well as the rebuilding of their Temple. No one was forced to go, as this was a decision each Jew was free to make for himself. Thus, it may be concluded by the mention of "survivors" in verse 4 that there

The Medo-Persian Empire, attributed largely to Cyrus the Great (550–530 B.C.), continued to expand even beyond his death. And up until that time, it was the largest empire in world history. Having conquered western Asia and Asia Minor, the empire also defeated Egypt in 535 B.C. Gradually, their control extended eastward toward the Indus River in India. The empire ceased to expand when the Greeks defeated them in the battle at Marathon in 490 B.C. Thus, the Medo-Persian Empire began to crumble when major parts of it were conquered by Alexander the Great from the year 334 until his death in 323 B.C. Among the things for which this empire is remembered are its administrative strength; good roads; the development of a shared, "universal" mindset among its peoples; and the prosperity its people enjoyed.

The books of Jeremiah and Isaiah contain many prophecies about the fall and destruction of Jerusalem, the Babylonian Exile, and the return of God's people after the Exile.

were indeed Jews who, for whatever reason, chose to stay in Babylon. While the term provides some ambiguity as to whether this is a reference solely to the Jews or all people who lived within Cyrus's domain, it is generally understood to mean those Jews who remained in the area. The fact that Cyrus would allow any Jew to return provided further encouragement on his part for the Jews to rebuild the Temple, as they would need to work together to accomplish this task. Harmony and unity were necessary to achieve a project of such magnitude.

Cyrus further gave his support by decreeing that those who chose to remain in Babylon make provisions for those who would return by supplying them with such things as "silver and gold, with goods and livestock, and with freewill offerings for the temple of God in Jerusalem" (v. 4). Not only would those who returned need items necessary for the Temple proper, but they would also need the means whereby to settle and establish themselves before undertaking the Temple project. The list of items given here seems to imply Cyrus's provision for such. In all likelihood, those who made the choice to go to Jerusalem gave up possessions and goods in order to make the arduous journey.

Sometimes God's work is beyond what one person alone can do. The challenge of the task necessitates that God's people work together to achieve the end result. We may be guilty of either trying to accomplish a monumental task on our own or perhaps watching others while they need our help to get a job done. What is God calling you to do at this moment?

■ *Cyrus decreed that the Jews could return to*
■ *Jerusalem and rebuild the Temple of the Lord*
■ *there.*

Judah's Return (1:5–11)

This section begins with the mention of family heads, priests, and Levites. These are representative of those who were influential as leaders among the Israelites. Interestingly, family heads are mentioned only in connection with the tribes of Judah and Benjamin. Since the empire of Cyrus also included what once had been Assyria, the nation which overtook the Northern Kingdom of Israel in 722/21 B.C., his edict was to the original twelve tribes. However, only Judah and Benjamin responded to his edict. These were the two tribes that composed the Southern Kingdom of Judah, the nation the Babylonians had exiled in 587/86 B.C.

Interesting to note is the author's mention *again* of God's divine intervention to prompt those who would return: "everyone whose heart God had moved—prepared to go up and build the house of the LORD in Jerusalem" (v. 5). Familial leadership—meaning the extended family or clan, (Judah and Benjamin)—and spiritual leadership (priests and Levites) comprised two significant areas of leadership within Jewish life.

One of the ironies of life is that to gain we must sometimes "give up" or release. It is easy to allow possessions and comfort to stand in the way of doing what God desires. However, greater blessings result when, with faith and commitment, we choose His way.

The mention of "neighbors" in verse 6 from the NIV is rendered "all those about them" in the NASB. Both translations seem to indicate a wider range of people than the Jewish relatives who would remain in the area. Whether Jew or not, those within the empire encouraged the Jews who would return by assisting them with gifts, goods, livestock, gold, silver, and offerings. Cyrus himself assisted them by "giving back" the Temple articles that Nebuchadnezzar had stolen from the Temple before it was burned.

Two persons are mentioned by name in verse 8: Mithredath, the treasurer of Persia, and Sheshbazzar, the prince of Judah. These also aided the Jews who returned. Specifically, Mithredath counted out to Sheshbazzar the items the Jews would receive.

Mithredath is a Persian name meaning "given by/to Mithra"; Mithra was a Persian god. *Sheshbazzar*, on the other hand, is a Babylonian name meaning "sin, protect the father" or "Shamash/Shashu, protect the father." Sin and Shamash/Shashu respectively are names of the moon god and sun god.

Some scholars have questioned whether Sheshbazzar was in actuality the man Zerubbabel. It was not uncommon for Jews to be given Babylonian names while they were in Babylon (note, for example, Dan. 1:7). Both men are mentioned as having served as governors. Additionally, both are said to have laid the Temple's foundation—compare Ezra 5:16 with Zechariah 4:9. For these reasons, some conclude that both names refer to one and the same person. Others, however, see Zerubbabel as a younger contemporary of Sheshbazzar. Still others would hold that Sheshbazzar and Zerubbabel were relatives, uncle and nephew, respectively. For those holding the latter two viewpoints, this would account for the difference in why both names are used within the biblical text.

As the inventory is taken, the items are counted as follows: gold dishes (30), silver dishes (1,000), silver pans (29), gold bowls (30), matching silver bowls (410), and other articles (1,000). Verse 11 states that the gold and silver items totaled 5,400. Sheshbazzar is mentioned here as having brought these to Jerusalem with the exiles who returned.

- *God's prophecy is fulfilled as the Jews are*
- *allowed to return to Jerusalem by the decree*
- *of King Cyrus of Persia.*

QUESTIONS TO GUIDE YOUR STUDY

1. Who prophesied that the Jews would be restored to Jerusalem after about seventy years?

2. What pagan ruler did God use to initiate the process of returning to Judah?

3. What does Ezra see as key motivation for those who returned to Jerusalem?
4. What does Cyrus give back to the Jews?

LIST OF THOSE WHO RETURNED (2:1–70)

Chapter 2 gives a methodical listing of the men who returned to Jerusalem from the Exile. These are even categorized according to various leadership responsibilities among the social structure of Hebrew life. Perhaps such a listing helped to give continuity and organization to those who traveled. Among other things, such a record gave evidence of those Jews who did indeed return. Furthermore, it gives evidence to God's fulfillment of His promise to the Jews.

Leadership and Family Heads (2:1–35)

This section begins with a word of introduction about those Jews who returned to Jerusalem and Judah. The writer takes a brief glance back in time to recall the captivity of the exiles by Nebuchadnezzar king of Babylon. In all likelihood, this helped to put the present situation in perspective for him and his readers, as the return was part of a larger picture for the Jews and God's plan for them. Interesting to note is that each person returned to his own city or town. This provides for some connectedness with Israel's past and God's purpose for His covenant people.

Verse 2 names Zerubbabel among other leaders with whom the Jews returned. The Nehemiah mentioned here is not the man of the book of Nehemiah. Although there are some differences (with names and numbers), this list parallels the list given in Nehemiah 7:6–73. Copying errors are usually blamed for the differences between the two.

The significance of families and individuals within God's plan is evidenced by the preservation of the names given within this list. For all practical purposes, Israel was dead—no longer a nation—once the people were taken into captivity. However, the detailing of names and the careful retention of them gives testimony to the fact that Israel was indeed alive at the most vital rung of society. God in His sovereignty was working to reestablish the nation once again—a nation comprised of individuals and family clans.

Verse 3 begins the actual list of family clans, the "men of the people of Israel." Eighteen of them are distinguished. Interestingly, verse 21 begins a list of geographical names, as opposed to people names. Why a listing of geographical names is not apparent, although speculations exist. Perhaps these were poorer Jews who had no land to claim in their name; perhaps they could only trace their lineage to a former city rather than a particular person. Whatever the reason, the author saw fit to connect these into the listing by geographical identification. Most of these are identified with the territory of Benjamin.

The priests were God's authorized representatives associated with the religious life which centered on the Temple. Only males could serve who were without physical defects and were direct descendants of Aaron, Israel's original high priest. In addition to their functions of administering over sacrifices and interpreting God's will, they provided religious instruction and pronounced God's blessings. Income was provided for them from the food sacrifices the Israelites brought before the Lord.

■ *Ezra categorized the list of the first group of*
■ *Jews who return to Jerusalem. Prominence is*
■ *given to those who lead the group including*
■ *the heads of family clans.*

Priests (2:36–39)

Those who served as priests within Israelite society played a significant role. Perhaps most distinctive was their function in relationship to the Old Testament sacrifices. They would minister before God and offer sacrifices upon the altar. Also associated with the priestly role was the interpretation of oracles. This was usually done by means of the lot (Urim and Thummim). Only those who were the descendants of Aaron could serve as priests.

Levites (2:40–42)

The office of priesthood was authorized through the tribe of Levi. Levi was Jacob's third son by his wife Leah. Since the priesthood in Israel represented the nation's relationship with God, His covenant, then, was mediated by means of the priesthood. In a symbolic way, the priests represented God's holiness and purity. Thus, the ultimate function of the Levites was that of helping Israel to be a holy people before God (note Num. 18:6).

Verses 41–42 mention additional personnel such as singers and gatekeepers. According to 2 Chronicles 5:13 the singers joined with trumpeters "as with one voice, to give praise and thanks to the LORD." King David told the Levites to appoint their relatives "as singers to sing joyful songs, accompanied by musical instruments" (1 Chron. 15:16).

Those who served as gatekeepers helped maintain the security of the Temple and its treasures at Jerusalem. As security officers they guarded all Temple entrances, secured the perimeter and storehouses of the Temple, and were responsible for opening and closing the Temple gates each day. King David originally selected certain individuals from the Levites to fulfill this duty (see 1 Chron. 23:5).

The Urim and Thummim were devices used by the priests to determine the will of God. Though little is known about them, they are believed to have been two small stones of different colors. They were carried in a pouch attached to the ceremonial garment of a Levitical priest from Aaron's family line (see Exod. 28:30). God's answer regarding a specific matter was believed to have been determined by whichever "stone" was either drawn out or shaken out.

The Levites were set aside by God for special worship-related service to Him. They were not directly related to Aaron but assisted their Aaronic relatives in offering the sacrifices and performing various rituals related to Israel's worship (see Num. 3:6, 9). They probably cared for the Temple and its sacred objects of worship (note Num. 3:7–8).

■ *Because of their specific role in relationship*
■ *to the Temple, priests and Levites were dis-*
■ *tinguished among those who returned to help*
■ *with the Temple's restoration.*

Temple Servants (2:43–54)

According to Ezra 8:20, Temple servants were given by David for the purpose of assisting the Levites. The Temple servants are believed to have been descendants of non-Israelites. It is possible that the list here could have included descendants of the Gibeonites. The book of Joshua records the story of how the Gibeonites tricked the Israelites and were, therefore, reduced to being their servants (see Josh. 9:27).

■ *Descendants of the Temple servants also*
■ *chose to return to Jerusalem.*

Descendants of Solomon's Servants (2:55–58)

The Temple servants of Solomon were probably non-Israelite descendants, those whom Solomon used as slaves. Since both groups (Solomon's servants and Temple servants) comprise one total here, they would be closely related. Again, perhaps Gibeonite descendants were among this group. The more mundane, day-to-day labor at the Temple would have included maintaining the supply of firewood and water. Although these groups were originally Canaanites, they would have become worshipers of God and, thus, would have been accepted by the Israelites and integrated into Jewish society.

■ *Descendants of the servants of Solomon, the*
■ *last king of all Israel, also returned to Jerus-*
■ *alem from the Exile.*

Uncertified Families (2:59–63)

Those identified with this list had no genealogical records. Verse 59 indicates they could provide no evidence of having descended from Israel. Reasons vary from that of these persons having lost their family records to the possibility of these being Jewish converts. The towns listed here were places in Mesopotamia where Jews had settled under Babylonian control.

The three families of priests mentioned in verse 61, Hobaiah, Hakkoz, and Barzillai, were also unable to provide genealogical proof of their ancestry. For this reason they were considered unclean and, therefore, excluded from the priesthood (v. 62). Furthermore, they were ordered not to eat the priestly portion of food from the sacrifices until a legitimate priest sought the Lord regarding the matter (see note on Urim and Thummim).

■ *Among those in Ezra's list of returnees are*
■ *Temple servants of non-Israelite background*
■ *and Jews who are unable to substantiate*
■ *their heritage, thus forfeiting their right to*
■ *the priesthood.*

Summary Totals (2:64–70)

As chapter 2 comes to a conclusion, totals on the whole assembly are given, even down to the animals the returnees took with them. This indicates the meticulousness with which the Jews kept their records. Verse 64 numbers 42,360 persons. This does not include servants and singers as mentioned in verse 65. Nehemiah 7:66 records the same total, as does the apocryphal book of 1 Esdras 5:41. There are, however, discrepancies when one seeks to add the totals given within each book. While the biblical account is trustworthy, explanations include the possibility of errors from copyists, the inclusion of women and/or children, the inclusion of unproven priests, or perhaps the inclusion of tribes other than Judah and Benjamin.

The mention of the animals here in addition to menservants and maidservants says something about the positive economic state of those who returned. Perhaps some of the animals were donated to the Jews by Cyrus (e.g., horses, which were associated with nobility).

Camels were a rarity in Israelite society. They were valuable mainly for merchants and military personnel because of their size and suitability for carrying loads on international routes in the open desert. The Israelites generally had no use for them because of their expense in upkeep and lack of agricultural value.

Once the Jews arrived in Jerusalem, some of the family heads voluntarily gave offerings for the express purpose of rebuilding the Temple on its previous site (compare with Neh. 7). The Temple personnel settled within the villages near Jerusalem. The rest of the Israelites settled in their towns within Judah. It is reasonable to conclude these settled where their families had lived prior to the Exile. God's promise to Israel was in the process of being realized.

- *The number of returnees within the first*
- *group to return to Jerusalem is specified as*
- *42,360 persons.*

QUESTIONS TO GUIDE YOUR STUDY

1. What were the significant roles of priests in Israel?
2. In addition to priests, what other personnel served in the Temple?
3. What was the Urim and Thummin?
4. Approximately how many Jews returned to Jerusalem in 538 B.C.?

THE REVIVAL OF TEMPLE WORSHIP (3:1–6:22)

Crucial to the re-establishment of the Jews in their homeland was their worship of God as it related to offerings and sacrifices. The carrying out of these would be fulfillment of the Law as given by God through Moses. The prophet Malachi called upon the Israelites to remember the Law upon their return. "Remember the law of Moses My servant, *even the* statutes and ordinances which I commanded him in Horeb for all Israel" (Mal. 4:4, NASB). The Law was just as applicable for the Israelites when they returned from captivity as it was during the time of Moses. Therefore, it was a vital part of the spiritual, economic, and sociological health and stability of the nation.

Rebuilding the Altar (3:1–3)

Once the Israelites had settled, they came together "as one man" in Jerusalem. The phrase "as one man" conveys the group's singleness of heart and purpose. They were united in their efforts to begin work on their Temple, which

The Israelites used two different calendars during the Old Testament period. One marked the religious year; the other, the civil year. The religious calendar began in the spring, commemorating Israel's Exodus from Egypt (see Exod. 12:2). The civil calendar's first month coincided with the seventh month of the religious year.

The feasts and sacred days which the Jews observed during the month of Tishri include the Feast of Trumpets/Jewish New Year (Rosh Hashanah), Numbers 29:1–6; the Day of Atonement (Yom Kippur), Leviticus 16:29–30; the Feast of Tabernacles, Deuteronomy 16:13–15; and the Sacred Assembly, Numbers 29:35–38.

Within the Law of Moses Israelite priests were required to offer sacrificial lambs to the Lord twice each day (see Exod. 29:39 and Num. 28:4).

was a necessary part in realizing their goal (see previous note on working together to accomplish God's work, sec. 1:2–4).

Interesting to note is the mention of the "seventh month." This would have been, according to the Jewish religious year, Tishri (September-October). This month was a holy and sacred month for the Jews (note Lev. 23:23–44).

Jeshua and Zerubbabel are mentioned in verse 2 among those leaders who helped build the altar for sacrificing burnt offerings in keeping with the Law of Moses. Though verse 3 indicates those participating in the project feared the people around them (the local residents), it is noteworthy that their fear did not keep them from building the altar. In spite of fear, and perhaps because of it, they were able to maintain their proper focus. Upon completion of the altar, morning and evening sacrifices were given.

■ *During the early fall of their first year back*
■ *in Jerusalem the Israelites rebuilt the Tem-*
■ *ple's sacrificial altar.*

Celebration, Offerings, and Sacrifices (3:4–7)

Careful to follow the Law's requirements, the Jews likewise celebrated the Feast of Tabernacles (also referred to as Booths or Ingathering) with its required number of daily offerings. They gave the regular burnt offerings and observed the New Moon sacrifices, as well as all the sacred feasts the Lord established. They even gave Him freewill offerings.

The manner in which all of this was done is a testimony to the peoples' attitude and concern toward worship. Remarkably, all this was done prior to having laid the foundation of the Temple. Further evidence of their generosity is seen in the provision of money for the masons and carpenters and food, drink, and oil for those who would bring cedar logs for the Temple.

■ *The Jews rebuilt the altar at Jerusalem and*
■ *joyfully celebrated giving God their offerings*
■ *and sacrifices.*

Rebuilding the Temple (3:8–6:22)

At last, work on the Temple became a reality. However, the Jews faced opposition in the process. The work came to a halt, but it later resumed. Included within this account are several letters which give insight regarding some of the obstacles the Jews faced and how God worked to overcome them. The Temple nevertheless was completed, and the Jews celebrated by observing Passover.

Restoration Begins (3:8–13)

Again the writer mentions specifically Zerubbabel and Jeshua as the two main leaders of the Temple project. Others are mentioned in a general sense: the priests, Levites, and those who came from captivity. The Levites who were twenty years of age and above were to oversee the project. Once the foundation was laid, the priests and Levites followed the directions earlier prescribed by King David in their praise to the Lord (see 1 Chron. 6:31). Music and musical instruments—trumpets and cymbals mentioned in verse 10—were a part of their praise. This verse also indicates the priests wore their priestly garments (note Exod. 28) for the

The Feast of Tabernacles (Hebrew "Sukkoth") was celebrated annually in the seventh month of the Jewish religious year. This served as a reminder of Israel's journey from Egypt to the Promised Land (see Lev. 23:43) as they celebrated the end of the agricultural harvest season (see Exod. 23:16; 34:22). Israelite families would live in temporary shelters made from palm fronds and willow branches.

The Israelites gave above and beyond what was required of them in their offerings and sacrifices. They also gave freewill offerings, offerings just because they wanted to give them. Sometimes we grumble and complain about giving a tithe to God. When was the last time you gave above and beyond, just for the sheer joy of giving? Giving voluntarily results from a thankful heart.

Music has always played an important role in worship. Before the time of the Temple, it was usually the women who sang and danced in a spontaneous way when the Israelites were victorious in battle (note Exod. 15:20–21; Judg. 11:34; and 1 Sam. 18:6–7). With the rise of the Temple, however, music became associated with the singers and players and was done in a more organized way. David, himself a gifted musician, appointed Levitical musicians who were responsible for vocal and instrumental music (see 1 Chron. 15:16). Music continues today to be a part of most worship services as a means of praising God and celebrating His wonderful blessings.

occasion. The people shouted as they proclaimed the Lord's goodness and His love! Truly it was a joyous event.

However, there were mixed emotions on this momentous occasion. While many rejoiced, and with good reason, those of the older generation were saddened as they remembered the previous Temple. Solomon's Temple had been a glorious Temple, and perhaps this celebration served to open the wounds associated with its earlier destruction. Expressions of both emotions were appropriate, as this was a bittersweet moment. So great was the noise from the commotion that no one could distinguish the cries from the shouts of joy. Furthermore, the noise could be heard for some distance. No doubt, others within the surrounding area were aware of this dramatic incident.

- *The completion of the Temple foundation*
- *was met with mixed emotions. Many rejoiced*
- *while others were saddened as they remem-*
- *bered the previous Temple.*

Work Threatened (4:1–7)

Word got around that the Jews were rebuilding the Temple. And when their enemies heard this, they approached Zerubbabel under the pretense of wanting to help and serve Israel's God. These "enemies" were people from Samaria who had been taken there under the Assyrian king Esarhaddon. However, the leaders of the project knew the intent of these enemies and would not allow them to help, citing they had nothing in common. At this the enemies resorted to tactics of discouragement, seeking to frighten the Jews, even to the point of hiring counselors to frustrate their plans. They did this throughout the reign of Cyrus until the reign of Darius.

Medo-Persian Kings During the Biblical Period

King	Dates
Cyrus the Great	550–531 B.C.
Cambyses	530–522 B.C.
Darius I	522–486 B.C.
Xerxes (Ahasuerus)	486–464 B.C.
Artaxerxes I	464–423 B.C.

Further opposition is seen during the reigns of the Persian kings Ahasuerus and Artaxerxes. The biblical account notes an accusation against Judah and Jerusalem during the reign of Ahasuerus (v. 6). The enemies continued their efforts against the Jews during the time of Artaxerxes by plotting against those at Jerusalem with a letter to him (v. 7). This was written in the official language of the day, Aramaic.

■ *Organized opposition soon arose to rebuild-*
■ *ing the Temple at Jerusalem; under Zerubba-*
■ *bel the Jews resisted.*

Letter to King Artaxerxes (4:8–16)

Verses 8–10 give something of an introduction regarding a letter to King Artaxerxes. The instigator of the letter is Rehum, who perhaps dictated it to his scribe Shimshai. Rehum had an official governmental role as he is referred to in

Esarhaddon was an aggressive Assyrian king who reigned from 681 to 669 B.C. following the death of his father Sennacherib (see 2 Kings 19:37). He is reputed to have marched his forces from the region of modern Iraq to northeast Africa in a conquest of Egypt and was responsible for forcing many non-Israelites to relocate to Samaria.

Although the Persians spoke the Persian language, Aramaic was the official language of the time, especially for correspondence within the Medo-Persian Empire. Being a North Semitic language, it was closely related to biblical Hebrew. Aramaic was eventually adopted as the primary language of many Jews. Jesus and Paul were among those who commonly spoke Aramaic in New Testament times.

verse 8 as the "commanding officer" (NIV) or "governor" (NLT). Some of his additional colleagues are mentioned by name in verse 9.

Rehum's letter refers to the Jews as rebellious in an effort to undermine the king's trust in them. Moreover, he spoke of their efforts in rebuilding the Temple and the walls around Jerusalem as being of evil intent. Furthermore, he cleverly brought up the matter of taxes and revenue by indicating the Jews, if allowed to continue in their rebuilding, would no longer render their loyalties to the king, thus posing a threat to his empire. Therefore, Rehum requested that a search be made of the empire's records to substantiate his claims. Further threat is given to King Artaxerxes in verse 16: "We declare that if this city is rebuilt and its walls are completed, the province west of the Euphrates River will be lost to you" (NLT).

■ *Enemies threatened any further work on the*
■ *Temple and sent a letter to King Artaxerxes*
■ *to halt the project.*

The King's Reply (4:17–23)

In all likelihood, the king was unable to read Aramaic. Verse 18 states the letter was translated and read to him. In the king's response to Rehum, he conveyed that a decree had been issued and a search made in keeping with his request. And since it had been found that the inhabitants of Jerusalem in times past revolted against other kingdoms, King Artaxerxes ordered that their work come to a halt until he issued another decree.

■ *In response to the letter from the Jews' oppo-*
■ *nents, King Artaxerxes ordered work on the*
■ *Temple to cease.*

Cessation of Work (4:24)

Work on the Temple ceased until the second year of the Persian king Darius (520 B.C.). The mention of King Darius occurs here in verse 24 as well as in verse 5, with other kings mentioned in between. Questions may arise as to the order in which they appear, since this chapter does not refer to them chronologically. Ezra summarized in verses 6–23 the account of the opposition to the Jews experienced as they rebuilt Jerusalem. A true chronological rendering would place 4:6 between chapters six and seven. No doubt, Ezra sought to highlight in a summative way the overall opposition which persisted throughout the years with more of a topical reference to these Persian kings.

■ *Work on the Temple ceased until 520 B.C.,*
■ *during the reign of King Darius.*

Building Resumes (5:1–2)

Haggai and Zechariah were prophets who sought to encourage the Jews in rebuilding the Temple. Ezra referred to them here as being a support to Zerubbabel and Jeshua during the period of Temple reconstruction. Not only did they encourage the builders through their words but by their participation in the labor as well (note also Hag. 1:13–14 and Zech. 4:6, 8–9).

The kingdom of God is more than a matter of words; it is the nitty-gritty of hard work. While words are cheap, our actions cost us time and effort and show our true commitment.

■ *During the time of Haggai and Zechariah, in*
■ *the second year of the Persian king Darius,*
■ *work resumed on the Temple.*

Opposition (5:3–17)

This section records the questioning of the Jews about the authority they had to rebuild the Temple. Tattenai, the present governor of the region, and his colleagues sent a letter to King Darius asking for verification of King Cyrus's decree permitting the Jews this privilege.

Jews Questioned (5:3–5). The governor of Trans-Euphrates at this point in time was Tattenai. His province would have included area west of the Euphrates River. The relationship of Shethar-Bozenai to Tattenai is uncertain, although some believe he could have been his secretary. They questioned the Jews about who had given them permission to rebuild the Temple. Revolts had been numerous during the first two years of Darius's reign, so their investigation into this matter was appropriate in light of their position and loyalty to the king. According to verse 4 the names of those who worked on the Temple had to be reported as part of the investigation.

In verse 5 the author gives credit to God for the fact that the Jews were allowed to continue with the project while the Persian officials awaited a word from the king. Tattenai seemingly had a positive attitude toward the Jews. He could have halted the project, as the writer knew full well. Yet Ezra saw in this God's providence, as did the people who continued their work on the Temple.

Adversaries' Letter to King Darius (5:6–17). Tattenai's letter to King Darius tells about his confronting the Jews about their rebuilding of the Temple. He questioned the Jews' authorization to rebuild and asked for a list of the names of those involved in the project. Verse 8 supplies some detail as to an inspection of the project with emphasis upon how well the Jews were progressing. Additionally, Tattenai included the Jews' response to his questioning.

The answer the Jews gave to Tattenai provided something of their history and God's claim upon them. They began their testimony by acknowledging their status as "servants of the God of heaven and earth" (v. 11). Israel's view of God was tied into her history. The Jews knew Him to be the sovereign creator and ruler over all. They also made reference here to a "great king of Israel" (meaning Solomon) under whom the first Temple was built, thus providing the context for their present efforts.

Admitting the sins of their ancestors against God, they went on to describe His judgment upon them through Nebuchadnezzar's destruction of the first Temple, including his removal of the Temple's gold and silver utensils and his deportation of their people to Babylon. They also spoke of Cyrus's decree, issued in his first year of reign over the Babylonians, which made allowance for them to rebuild their Temple. Having relayed this information to King Darius, Tattenai requested that a search be made to find this decree of Cyrus and that word be sent back to him regarding the matter.

Consistently the Old Testament taught that Israel's sins would be punished by enemy attacks and the defeat of her nation. This theme first appeared in the Law of Moses (Lev. 26:17 and Deut. 28:25), was reinforced in the prophets (Jer. 4:6; Amos 3:10–14; and Hab. 1:6), and demonstrated in the history of Israel (Judg. 2:14; 4:2; 6:1; 2 Kings 24:2; and Dan. 1:2).

- *The Jews were questioned by Tattenai the*
- *governor as to their permission to rebuild the*
- *Temple. This resulted in a letter to King Dar-*
- *ius.*

King Darius's Response (6:1–12)

The decree of Cyrus was discovered, and King Darius sent Tattenai his reply. His response not only relayed what was contained within Cyrus's decree but also included a decree of his own which allowed the Jews to continue their work.

Search for the Decree of Cyrus (6:1–5). Under the orders of King Darius, a search was made in keeping with Tattenai's request for the Cyrus decree within the Babylonian archives. Interestingly, the scroll containing the decree was not found there but rather in Ecbatana. Ecbatana was one of four capital cities within the Persian Empire. Just as the Jews had asserted, so was the message of the decree. While additional information is given here regarding Temple measurements and the number of layers for stones and timbers, King Darius quoted from Cyrus's decree saying, "Let the temple be rebuilt . . . and let its foundations be laid" (v. 3). Verse 5 mentions the Temple vessels: "the gold and silver articles of the house of God . . . are to be returned to their places in the temple." Moreover, Cyrus decreed the expenses be paid for by the royal treasury.

Ecbatana was the capital of the ancient Median Empire prior to Cyrus the Great's conquest of Media. The city was made a provincial capital in the Persian Empire following the defeat of the Medes. One of four Persian capitals (the others being Babylon, Persepolis, and Susa), it was located in the Zagros mountains of western Iran beneath the modern city of Hamadan.

Order to Rebuild (6:6–12). With the reply of Darius came the order for Tattenai and his colleagues to leave the work alone. Verse 6 even orders them to "stay away from there!" (NLT). They were not to disturb the Temple's construction nor hinder the governor in the work being done. Furthermore, Darius issued his own proclamation regarding the project, stating Tattenai was to provide fully for the Jews' expenses. This was to be taken from area taxes stored within the royal treasury. Darius even made arrangements for providing the Jews acceptable items for their sacrifices. This was to be done on a daily basis.

History reveals that the Persian rulers were quite favorable toward the foreign religions and cults represented within their empire. Among the reasons included the possible prayers on behalf of the kings to the various gods. Thus, the rulers took seriously their subjects' religious practices. Darius admitted this in giving reason to Tattenai for the provisions of Israel's offerings: "that they may . . . pray for the well-being of the king and his sons" (v. 10).

Not only did the king dictate these things, but he also released another decree stating the consequences of anyone who might violate the edict. According to verse 11 the violator's house would become a "pile of rubble" (NLT) or a "refuse heap" (NASB), and a beam from it would be used as a means for his own torturous death. Moreover, he called upon Israel's God to bring down any king or people who endeavored to change it. Reference to the God who "caused his Name to dwell there" (v. 12) seems to support the theological claim of a Jewish scribe who, perhaps, assisted King Darius in the preparation of this decree.

The support of the Persian kings toward their subjects' religious practices are remarkable. Even more so was their knowledge of these practices. Aside from biblical insights, nonbiblical sources show that Temples were repaired by Cyrus at Uruk and Ur. Additionally, Cambyses provided funds for the Sais Temple, and Darius ordered the Temple of Amun rebuilt.

The process of impaling was used in ancient Mesopotamia as a common means of execution. A pole was planted into the ground, and the criminal's body was forced down upon it, thus "piercing" his body. Often the condemned criminal's house would also be destroyed (note Dan. 2:5).

■ *The search for Cyrus's decree was met with*
■ *success, and King Darius gave orders for the*
■ *Jews to continue rebuilding their Temple.*

The Temple Completed (6:13–15)

Having received the reply from King Darius, Tattenai and Shethar-Bozenai complied with his mandate. So the Jewish leaders continued in their work with the encouragement of Haggai and Zechariah. They met with success as the Temple was completed in the sixth year of Darius's reign (516 B.C.) on the third day of Adar (February-March). Thus, God's command was fulfilled in addition to the decrees of the Persian kings Cyrus, Darius, and Artaxerxes.

■ *The Jews completed the Temple of the Lord at*
■ *Jerusalem in 516 B.C.*

Celebration (6:16–22)

The Temple's completion was a notable accomplishment for the Israelite community. They were able to realize their goal after having faced obstacles that threatened not only the project's completion but their lives as well. They dedicated the Temple with joy and celebrated by giving various offerings and observing Passover. God's provision and protection had brought them to this climatic and historic event.

Dedication of the Temple (6:16–18). The celebration at the Temple's dedication was a community affair. Leadership, represented by the priests and Levites, as well as the people at large gathered to rejoice and worship God. Bulls, rams, lambs, and goats were offered to the Lord. A comparison of this dedication to the dedication of Solomon's Temple reveals the "hundreds" of animals sacrificed here to be smaller than the "thousands" sacrificed during the dedication of the first Temple (see 1 Kings 8:63). However, this was no less an ardent undertaking.

Included as part of this latter dedication was the sin offering, which utilized twelve goats corresponding to the twelve tribes of Israel. Additionally, the priests and Levites were commissioned to their respective divisions for service at the Temple as the Book of Moses prescribed. (See 1 Chron. 24:1–19. There were twenty-four separate priestly divisions.)

Verse 18 concludes the Aramaic portion. Consequently, verse 19 resumes in the Hebrew.

Observance of Passover (6:19–22). Among the most significant observances of the Jews included Passover. Having its roots in the Exodus experience, it marked the deliverance of the Israelites from Egyptian bondage. In Exodus 12:14 the Jews are commanded, "You must remember this day forever. Each year you will celebrate it as a special festival to the LORD" (NLT). According to Exodus 12:6 Passover was to be celebrated on the fourteenth day of the first month of Israel's religious year (Nisan, March-April). These former exiles were careful to observe it on the designated day in keeping with the Law. In a symbolic way, the Israelites were free from bondage once again, the bondage of Exile. Their Temple was now complete, and it served as a visual symbol of that freedom.

A part of the Passover observance included the purification of the priests and Levites. In order

The sacrifice for Israel's sin offering varied depending upon who committed the sin. For example, a bull was required if a priest or the congregation sinned. A ruler could bring a male goat, whereas most others could use female goats or lambs. Provision was made for the poor by the acceptance of two turtledoves or, in extreme cases, a tenth of an ephah of flour. In so doing, the violator was "purified" from unintentional sin. Leviticus 4 gives further information on the sin offering.

The essence of true worship genuinely seeks to do things God's way. The Jews were careful to observe Passover according to the Law. Christian worship also delights in fulfilling God's requirements as it remembers what He has done for us and celebrates His goodness.

Passover, the first of three annual festivals among the Jews, commemorates God's protection and deliverance of the Israelites from Egyptian slavery. The death of the firstborn was the last of ten plagues God sent to persuade the Egyptians to free the Israelites. The Israelites were spared this plague by the spreading of blood from a Passover lamb upon their doorposts. After they had eaten the Passover meal in haste, God miraculously led the Israelites to freedom as He parted the Red Sea for their crossing. The Egyptians were drowned as they followed in hot pursuit after the Israelites. Exodus 11–14 give greater background and meaning to the Passover experience.

We tend to spend time with those who are like us. However, the kingdom of God is not limited to one kind of group, be it race, age, gender, status, or interest. Because God accepts all those who love and serve Him—no matter how different they may be—so should we.

to fulfill their priestly duties, the Law required them to be ceremonially clean. This was done by a ceremonial washing (see Exod. 29:4 and Num. 8:7). In this way they were "pure" before God to fulfill the role for which He ordained them. This included slaughtering the Passover lamb by the Levites for all the exiles, additional priests, and themselves.

Those who participated in the Passover meal and celebration also included "others in the land who had turned from their immoral customs to worship the LORD, the God of Israel" (v. 21, NLT). This is a reference to the Jews who had lived in Judah and had integrated with non-Jews. The willingness of the former exiles to accept these repentant pagans shows remarkable efforts at fostering community, while at the same time fulfilling the demands of the Law.

The Jews also expressed their joy by observing the Feast of Unleavened Bread for a period of seven days. Although this feast and Passover were originally separate holy occasions, they became inseparable due to their close time proximity.

■ *With God's help the Jerusalem Temple was*
■ *completed. The Jews celebrated by dedicat-*
■ *ing the Temple and observing Passover.*

QUESTIONS TO GUIDE YOUR STUDY

1. How does Ezra describe the manner in which the people came together to build the Temple?

2. Who were the two key leaders in the construction of the Temple?

3. What two emotions were expressed when the foundation of the Temple was laid?

4. What caused the work on the Temple to come to a halt?

EZRA'S RETURN (7:1–8:36)

Approximately fifty-seven years had passed at this point since the completion of the Temple. The man for whom the book is named was among a second group of exiles who returned to Jerusalem in 458 B.C. This section includes Ezra's genealogy, a detailing of King Artaxerxes' letter to Ezra, a list of those who accompanied Ezra, Ezra's request for Levites and proclamation of a fast, and information regarding Temple treasures.

Ezra's Genealogy (7:1–6)

The listing of Ezra's ancestors traces him to the priestly line of Aaron. Ezra, in supplying his genealogy, gave documentation of his priesthood as well as substantiation of his return to Jerusalem. Reference to his skill as a scribe is also given. Among the most striking claims was his admission of God's favor upon him. He saw the courtesy of King Artaxerxes toward him as part of this favor. "The king granted him all he requested" (v. 6, NASB).

■ *Ezra documented his priestly heritage and*
■ *the fact that the favor of God was upon him.*

Background Information (7:7–10)

These verses give some detail regarding those who came with Ezra to Jerusalem and the timing of the journey. Mention is made of priests, Levites, singers, gatekeepers, and Temple

Genealogies were important in Israelite society. They helped establish a person's credibility and indicated his significance within the community. The larger one's genealogy, the more credible and significant he was. The person the Bible records with the longest genealogy is Jesus Christ. He can be traced through seventy-six generations back to Adam (see Luke 3:23–38). Ezra, by contrast, went back sixteen generations to the high priest Aaron.

The term *scribe* in the Old Testament refers to one who served as a king's secretary (note 2 Kings 22:3) as well as one who was trained in writing skills (note Jer. 36:32). Scribes who copied and preserved the Scriptures, such as Ezra, became experts in and, therefore, teachers of the Law. This characterized the time of the Exile.

servants—personnel who assisted in some way with worship at the Temple. They came to Jerusalem in King Artaxerxes' seventh year. The arrival time was the first day of the fifth month (Ab, July-August). Departure had taken place on the first day of the first month. Again, the writer speaks of God's blessing. The phrase "for the gracious hand of his God was on him" (v. 9) is used. Verse 10 explains that Ezra was blessed because he had committed himself to the diligent study, observance, and teaching of the Law.

■ *When Ezra returned to Jerusalem with a sec-*
■ *ond group of Exiles, he validated his right to*
■ *be among the returnees by providing his*
■ *genealogy and acknowledging God's*
■ *goodness.*

Decree of Artaxerxes (7:11–26)

The generosity of King Artaxerxes was expressed in his letter, written in Aramaic, which permitted Ezra and the Temple personnel to return to Jerusalem. They were given silver and gold and were even assisted by area treasurers as mandated by the king. Ezra was also authorized to avail himself of the royal treasury as was needed.

Persons Allowed to Return with Ezra (7:11–14)

The letter the king gave to Ezra recognized his role as priest and teacher of God's Law. He extended cordial greetings and gave permission for Ezra and any priest and Levite who so desired to go to Jerusalem with the backing of his council of seven men. They placed full confidence in Ezra and his ability to teach the Law of God.

Provisions of Gold and Silver (7:15–20)

King Artaxerxes and his men donated gifts to God of gold and silver. Additionally, the king granted Ezra permission to obtain silver and gold from the people within the province of Babylon. Furthermore, freewill offerings were given with the understanding that these monies would be used for buying the needed items for sacrifices at the Temple. Although the Jews took with them various articles for worship, they would need to purchase such things as animals and grain required for sacrifices. The king trusted Ezra to use any remaining gold and silver as he deemed necessary. Likewise, he was authorized to obtain monies from the royal treasury for any further needs.

The Mandate for Help from Area Treasurers (7:21–24)

God's goodness and providence are seen further with the king's mandate to all the treasurers of the Trans-Euphrates province to supply whatever Ezra needed. Up to "a hundred talents of silver" (v. 22) alone, not to mention measures of wheat, wine, oil, and the like, seems rather exorbitant. Although limits are placed upon the various items listed, the generosity of the king is astounding.

King Artaxerxes was careful to supply Ezra with all that God required. "Whatever the God of heaven has prescribed, let it be done with diligence" (v. 23). He did not want to invoke the wrath of God upon himself or his family line. Coupled with this, he granted the Temple personnel exemption from the payment of

The gifts and abilities which God grants individuals are generally recognized and affirmed by others. This is especially true among the community of believers. Ezra had so distinguished himself that even the pagan King Artaxerxes recognized his abilities. Are you faithful to use your gifts and abilities for God's kingdom? Do you help encourage and affirm others where God has gifted them?

taxes—not an uncommon practice among the Persians.

■ *King Artaxerxes supported the return of*
■ *Ezra, the priests, and Levites to Jerusalem by*
■ *his provision of gold and silver and man-*
■ *dated aid from area treasurers.*

Royal Authority Granted to Ezra (7:25–26)

God's providential hand is seen again in the king's authorization of Ezra to appoint judicial leaders among the Jews. He recognized Ezra's giftedness and ability; therefore, he sanctioned him to give leadership over those within the Trans-Euphrates province. There is some question as to the interpretation of verse 25. Does the phrase "all who know the laws of your God" refer to those *who rule* or those *who are ruled*? This raises some question about those over whom Ezra had jurisdiction. It is unclear whether this included non-Jews. What is clear is that the king knew Ezra to be capable of leadership and associated this with God and His Law.

The king encouraged Ezra to teach God's laws to those who were unfamiliar with them. Failure to keep them, or the king's laws, would result in death, banishment, confiscation, or imprisonment.

Ezra's Praise to God (7:27–28)

Ezra recognized that it was God who had worked within the king to bring about his kindnesses and favor toward the Jews and their Temple. Therefore, he praised the Lord, which is a fitting response to God's goodness, providence, and faithfulness. Assurance of His presence and

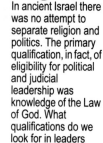

In ancient Israel there was no attempt to separate religion and politics. The primary qualification, in fact, of eligibility for political and judicial leadership was knowledge of the Law of God. What qualifications do we look for in leaders today? Does this comply with God's standards?

blessing had given Ezra hope and encouragement in an otherwise futile situation.

■ *The king, aware of Ezra's skill in leadership*
■ *ability, authorized him to provide leadership*
■ *over the Trans-Euphrates province. Ezra*
■ *knew God to be in this and praised Him*
■ *accordingly.*

List of Those Returning with Ezra (8:1–14)

Within this section Ezra listed those who accompanied him to Jerusalem. The attention to family heads here stresses the importance of the communal aspect of the Jewish people and their heritage. God had called them as a nation and had covenanted with them to be His people. His blessing was upon them as He used the nation as a whole, as well as tribes and clans, for His specific purposes. Once again God worked through these families to bring about blessing and the fulfillment of His purposes as they left Babylon to go to Jerusalem.

This list is different from those of Ezra 2 and Nehemiah 7. Some account for the difference by saying this list was meant to give legitimacy to the genealogies of those who traveled with Ezra. Women and children are not included in the 1,496 total. The descendants of fifteen individuals are highlighted here.

■ *A total of 1,496 individuals from fifteen dif-*
■ *ferent families were among those returning*
■ *to Jerusalem.*

So often it is easy to forget that God deserves and inhabits the praise of His people. Ezra gave credit where credit was due. How often do you stop to praise and thank God for His goodness and faithfulness to you?

God still uses families today. This includes not only the immediate family but the larger context of the generations, i.e., grandparents, great-grandparents, great-great-grandparents as well. While modern-day families have limited the significance associated with the larger family structure in practice, it is the connection with our larger family context which provides us a sense of identity and heritage—physically and spiritually.

Ezra Sends for Levites (8:15–20)

The "Ahava Canal" is mentioned in verse 15. This spot is singled out as a place where the Jews stopped to camp for three days. While here, Ezra analyzed the situation and discovered no Levites among their group. He sent eleven men to Iddo, the leader of the Levites at Casiphia, to ask for assistance in sending back ministers to serve at the Temple.

In all likelihood, the Ahava River was located near Babylon. While the exact site is unknown, it probably flowed into the Tigris or Euphrates river.

A common phrase used within the book of Ezra is "the gracious hand of our God was on us." Ezra once again used it in this situation (v. 18). The bringing of Sherebiah, Hashabiah, Jeshaiah, and some of their relatives evidence God's provision for them. Along with these approximately forty men, there were also 220 Temple servants who responded to Ezra's plea.

Aside from its mention in Ezra 8:17, there are no further biblical references to Casiphia (meaning "silversmith"). The Levites had settled here during the Exile.

■ *Ezra's spiritual sensitivity was demonstrated*
■ *as he sent representatives to appeal to Levites*
■ *to join with their group.*

Prayer and Fasting (8:21–23)

A part of Ezra's skillful leadership and organization was his proclamation and observance of a fast. The purpose of the fast was so the Jews could humble themselves and petition God's protection for a safe journey. Ezra realized the importance of seeking God's guidance and help for the journey.

Fasting is voluntarily refusing to eat for a period of time. As practiced by people in the Bible, it was a powerful religious act. By combining fasting with humility and prayer, people expressed that they were more concerned about seeking God and the blessings of a relationship with Him than in satisfying a bodily appetite.

Part of Ezra's concern was the king's view of God. Ezra had claimed that God would bless those who honored Him and be angry with those who turned away from Him. Ezra's admission of being ashamed to approach the king for military protection in verse 22 is a testimony to his dependance upon God. He was willing to risk trusting God rather than trusting the king, knowing God's reputation was at stake. Indeed, verse 33 reports that God answered their prayer.

■ *Before the journey began, Ezra led the people*
■ *to fast and rely upon God for protection dur-*
■ *ing their travel.*

Administrative Assignments (8:24–30)

After the fast Ezra chose twelve leaders of the priests, among whom were Sherebiah and Hashabiah, to transport the gold, silver, and other items that had been given for the Temple. They were to guard these treasures with diligence and bring them safely to Jerusalem. Ezra weighed the treasures and found there to be 24 tons of silver; an additional 7,500 pounds of silver utensils; 7,500 pounds of gold; 20 gold bowls valued at 19 pounds; and 2 polished bronze articles as precious as gold.

Ezra encouraged the priests by reminding them that the Temple items were holy before God. The priests accepted the challenge before them and took the items from the Ahava River to Jerusalem.

■ *Ezra entrusted valuable gifts for the Temple*
■ *to twelve men who were responsible for*
■ *transporting them safely to Jerusalem.*

The Journey to Jerusalem (8:31–36)

The record of the Jews' arrival in Jerusalem is mentioned with yet another reference to God's

Do you seek God's guidance and protection in travel? Ezra knew the value of petitioning God in such matters, not only for the potential outcome for him and his fellow Jews but for the witness and testimony this served for others as well, particularly the king. Despite what we may think, our actions and attitudes do affect others' view of God.

The amount of gold and silver brought to the Temple exceeded the amount given by the Israelites for the construction of the tabernacle in Moses' day. The 603,550 males in Moses' day gave about 7,545 pounds of silver and 2,200 pounds of gold (note Exod. 38:24–25).

blessing. "The gracious hand of our God protected us and saved us from enemies" (v. 31, NLT). Here they rested for three days before placing the articles in the Temple. These were weighed again in the Temple and entrusted to Meremoth, perhaps the high priest, and other Temple personnel. The former Exiles then offered burnt offerings to the Lord. Afterwards they delivered the letter of King Artaxerxes to his officials. With this, the Jews had the full support of the Persians to live and worship in their original homeland.

■ *Because of God's blessing the Jews and all*
■ *their valuable offerings for the Temple*
■ *arrived safely in Jerusalem. Once there they*
■ *worshiped God and delivered royal orders.*

QUESTIONS TO GUIDE YOUR STUDY

1. When did Ezra return from captivity to Jerusalem?
2. Describe the circumstances that came together allowing Ezra to return.
3. What did Ezra do in preparation for the journey to Jerusalem?
4. What was the first priority of those who returned to Jerusalem?

EZRA'S REFORMS (9:1–10:44)

This section deals with the Jews' problem of mixed marriages. A list is given of those who had violated God's law by marrying foreigners. Ezra led the people to confess their sin before God and rectify the situation.

The Problem of Mixed Marriages (9:1–4)

Once the Jews were somewhat settled within the area, the Jewish leaders approached Ezra with the admission of having violated God's command not to intermarry with other nations. Interestingly, it was the leaders who took the initiative in approaching Ezra. Many explain this to be because of Ezra's diligent teaching of the Law. True confession begins with acknowledgment of one's sins. Not only had many of the people intermarried, but those who served as their priests and Levitical leaders had also. Thus, Israel had adopted the sinful ways of the Canaanites (see those mentioned in v. 1). God's chosen people, a holy race, were no different than the pagans around her.

Ezra responded to the situation expressing outward signs of humiliation and grief. "When I heard this, I tore my tunic and cloak, pulled hair from my head and beard and sat down appalled" (v. 3). In all likelihood, Ezra knew about the situation prior to the leaders' coming to him. However, at this point he was moved to express in a solemn, yet visible way the seriousness of the situation. He sat in self-abasement until it was time for the evening sacrifice, while others who took seriously God's Law gathered around him.

The Israelites had intermarried with the Canaanites, the pagan nations around Israel, since the days of the judges. God through Moses warned the Israelites before entering the Promised Land not to integrate in any way with these nations (see, for example, Exod. 34:11–16 and Deut. 7:1–4). In fact, they were commanded to destroy them totally (note Deut. 7:2). The problem was not intermarriage in and of itself; idolatry was the ultimate issue.

- Ezra expressed grief over the sinful inter-
- marriage of Jews with non-Jews in Judah.

Ezra's Prayer of Confession (9:5–15)

At the designated time for the evening sacrifice, Ezra prayed earnestly to God. His attitude of contrition was conveyed even in his posture, as he fell on his knees and spread out his hands before God. His body as well as his spirit showed humility.

The remnant mentioned in Ezra 9:8 was given stability and permanence upon returning to Jerusalem. Because of God's grace Israel was given a "peg" (NASB), a "nail" (KJV), a "firm place" (NIV), and "security" (NLT). The prophet Isaiah spoke of Jerusalem's security in 33:20–21. Jerusalem is referred to as "a tent that will not be moved; its stakes will never be pulled up, nor any of its ropes broken. There the LORD will be our Mighty One" (NIV).

Ezra points us to a sobering reality; true repentance calls for the *specific confession* of sin against holy God. In a day and age where rights tend to take precedence over responsibility, this is a needed reminder. Sin cannot be taken lightly. Genuine confession begins with shame and embarrassment over our sin. How do you respond to and deal with sin?

An analysis of Ezra's prayer reveals something of his character and integrity. Ezra first of all expressed shame and embarrassment over having sinned. He would not so much as lift his face toward God. He realized the seriousness of disobedience against God. Second, there was the admission of sin in its magnitude. This expressed itself in the phrase "our sins are higher than our heads" (v. 6). Third, there was the recognition of a broader pattern of sin. Israel was linked to ancestors who also sinned against God and suffered judgment—judgment which continued to affect the present-day Jews. Fourth, although there was judgment, Ezra recognized God's grace in the firm restoration of Israel's remnant. God's enduring love extended to her through the actions of the Persian kings. This resulted in renewed joy and vigor for Israel with the restoration of the Temple and city walls.

As Ezra continued his prayer, he repeated in a summative way God's command and warning against intermarriage. In so doing, he acknowledged specific sin in his confession. He realized that God's judgment on the nation had been the result of sin. And, though the Jews stood guilty, God had not punished them as they had deserved. If He had, Israel would no longer exist. God's mercy had sustained Israel and elevated the nation to a status of privilege.

Another part of Ezra's prayer declared God as righteous. Israel needed to be reminded of God's righteousness and their failure to measure up to His standards. Because God is righteous, He punishes. However, it was God's righteousness that also preserved the remnant.

- *Ezra responded to the peoples' sin with*
- *shame, humility, and prayerful confession*
- *of sin.*

The People's Response (10:1–6)

As Ezra offered his prayer of confession at the Temple, many of the men, women, and children gathered around him and wept with him. The manner in which Ezra conducted himself, no doubt, attracted the attention of many people. However, those mentioned here were conscience stricken along with Ezra, as is evidenced by the phrase "wept bitterly." Shecaniah spoke up to declare for the group that they had been unfaithful to God by marrying the foreign women. Yet, he knew there was hope with repentance. Thus, he proposed they make a covenant with God to rectify the situation by sending away their pagan wives and children. Divorce, then, became part of the covenant agreement in an effort to bring the community in line with God's Law. Ezra was encouraged to lead as Shecaniah pledged the people's support.

Ezra, therefore, urged all Israel, including the priests and Levites, to fulfill the covenant Shecaniah had proposed. And they did so. As Ezra left the front of the Temple, he continued to fast. He was willing to follow through in private with what he had done in public. This demonstrated his authenticity in confession.

- *Ezra led the Jews to make a covenant to*
- *repent and dissolve their sinful marriages.*

The word *covenant* means agreement or testament. Different types of covenants are represented throughout the Bible and begin as early as the book of Genesis. Generally speaking, covenants were treaties between two parties either of equal or unequal authority and were legally binding. Penalties were usually associated with the failure to comply with covenant stipulations.

Assemblage for Investigation and Covenant Renewal (10:7–17)

The Jews were given three days to prepare and come together for the covenant. The seriousness with which this agreement was taken may be seen in the penalty established for the failure to show up during the designated three-day period. Those who failed to do so would forfeit their property and the right to be included among the assembly of the Exiles.

The Jews came together on the twentieth day of the ninth month (Kislev, November-December), which is normally part of Israel's rainy season. As the Jews gathered, the rains poured. While the weather caused the people to tremble, the solemn occasion, no doubt, added to their anxiety.

Generally, Israel's year may be divided into two major weather patterns: rainy and dry. The rainy season began around mid-October and lasted through April. The month of Kislev fell during this period and would account partly for the cold and damp experience of the Jews as they gathered.

Ezra reminded the people how they had violated God's Law by intermarrying with the pagans. He urged them to confess their wrongdoing and act upon that confession by separating themselves from their foreign wives. Those who gathered pledged to do so, knowing this was their responsibility. However, they were also aware of the magnitude of their decision; it could not be done in a matter of a few days and under the duress of the heavy rains. Therefore, they suggested their leaders set up designated times for them to come back and deal with the matter in a God-pleasing way. Four persons—Jonathan, Jahzeiah, Meshullam, and Shabbethai—are mentioned as having opposed this suggestion. However, with the backing of the Exiles, Ezra selected family heads to investigate the cases. This took approximately three months, having begun on the first day of the tenth month (Tebet, December-January) and concluding on the first day of the first month (Nisan, March-April).

- *The spiritual example set forth by Ezra*
- *prompted the people to correct the problem*
- *of sinful marriages.*

List of Those Found Guilty (10:18–44)

The concluding section of the book of Ezra lists those who had married foreign women. Among these are several priests, one singer, and three gatekeepers. Verse 19 indicates they pledged (literally, "gave their hands") to put away their wives. This perhaps was a symbolic handshake or gesture which sealed the pledge. Further evidence of their sincerity may be seen in the offering of rams for their guilt.

Although children had resulted from many of the marriages to these pagans, this was not reason enough for the Israelites to remain married to them. Implied here is that the children were also sent away. While divorce is never God's ideal, it may be the lesser of two evils, as was the case in the book of Ezra. Idol worship was far worse than divorcing these pagans. Left to its logical conclusion, it would have ultimately destroyed the restored Jewish community and, thus, God's special plan for them.

Israel's guilt offering is difficult to distinguish from her sin offering. The guilt offering has been described as a type of sin offering and was often associated with restitution. Usually a ram was required, although some other animals were permitted (see Lev. 5).

- *Ezra presented evidence of the sin of inter-*
- *marriage by listing the names of those who*
- *were guilty.*

QUESTIONS TO GUIDE YOUR STUDY

1. What practice among God's people grieved Ezra?
2. How did Ezra show his grief and sorrow?
3. What did the people do when they realized they were out of God's will?
4. Define *covenant*.

NEHEMIAH

NEHEMIAH'S CONCERN OVER JERUSALEM (1:1–2:10)

The book of Nehemiah complements the book of Ezra. Whereas Ezra was especially concerned to rebuild the spiritual walls of Jerusalem—that is, to bring Israel back to obedience of the Law of Moses, Nehemiah was especially interested in rebuilding the physical walls of Jerusalem. Ezra emphasized the religious dimensions of building a nation; Nehemiah emphasized the political and military dimensions of the task.

This section of the book of Nehemiah follows the account of how Nehemiah, a Jew who was an important official in the ancient Persian Empire, was inspired to help rebuild the walls of Jerusalem, the capital city of his ancestors' nation. As in the book of Ezra, God worked in the heart of a pagan king (Artaxerxes) to support Nehemiah in his divinely mandated task.

News from Jerusalem (1:1–3)

Nehemiah's story begins in the month of Kislev (November-December) during the twentieth year of the reign of the Persian king Artaxerxes I in 446 B.C. Nehemiah was serving as one of the king's trusted personal attendants at the royal palace in Susa.

Susa was the winter capital of the ancient Persian Empire. Its ruins are located in what is today southwestern Iran. Susa is also mentioned within the book of Esther in reference to the rule of the Persian king Xerxes.

Nehemiah received a visit from a group of men which included his brother Hanani. The men had just completed a journey of almost eleven hundred miles, having arrived from the Persian province of Judah. Nehemiah plied the travelers with questions regarding the Jewish community living in Judah, as well as questions about Jerusalem.

Verse 3 indicates that Nehemiah learned things were not going well for the Jews in their homeland. They were facing hardships and humiliation from non-Jewish settlers who were living in the area. In addition, Jerusalem's defenses—her walls and gates—remained in ruins, despite the fact that Jews had been living in the city for more than ninety years. Jerusalem's wooden city gates, the closeable passageways through the city wall, had not been repaired since they were burned by the Babylonians in 586 B.C., some 140 years earlier.

■ *Nehemiah was saddened as he learned the*
■ *news about the ruined walls and gates of*
■ *Jerusalem from his brother Hanani and the*
■ *men from Judah.*

Nehemiah's Prayer and Concern (1:4–11)

Nehemiah provided a touching and godly response to the troubling news he received from the delegation from Jerusalem. Apparent is Nehemiah's devotion to God and his desire to help his fellow Jews. He sought God's help after confessing sin against Him.

In Exodus 3:14 God revealed His covenantal name to Moses—"I AM THE ONE WHO ALWAYS IS" (NLT). God reminded Moses here of His covenant promises by referring to Abraham, Isaac, and Jacob—the ancestors of Moses. God is unchanging and fulfills His promises.

Confession of Sins (1:4–7)

Nehemiah's first response to the disheartening news regarding Jerusalem and its Jewish inhabitants was great sadness. Setting aside concern for the dignity of his position within the royal administration, Nehemiah immediately sat down and began to weep aloud. So troubling was the news that it disrupted his normal daily routine for several days. During that time he mourned and refused to eat.

Coupled with his fast, Nehemiah also prayed. In his prayer Nehemiah first identified the *One* to whom he was praying. Nehemiah called God by His covenantal name—the LORD or Yahweh (v. 5). The use of this name affirms the fact that God is a living being, a dynamic personality who has reached out and acted in behalf of His people in the past. Second, Nehemiah spoke of "the God of heaven" (vv. 4–5). Nehemiah knew that God was not bound by His created order. God is big enough to handle even the biggest of earth's problems. Next, Nehemiah confessed that his God was a promise-keeping God, one whose most basic attribute is love (v. 5).

Early on in the prayer, Nehemiah admitted to God that both he and his ancestors had acted in a way that was undeserving of any gift of God's love. Instead of showing loving obedience to God, he and generations of other Israelites had acted wickedly and rebelliously, refusing to obey God's Word given to Moses.

Request for God's Help (1:8–11)

Referring to statements found in the Law of Moses (Lev. 26:33 and Deut. 30:4), Nehemiah reminded God that He had made two declarations to the Israelites. First, God had warned His people He would punish them for their sins. If Israel persisted in unfaithfulness to God, He would scatter the Jews among the nations. And God had kept His word.

Second, Nehemiah reminded God that He had promised to bring the Israelites back to Israel from all over the world when they repented of their sins and obeyed Him. Among other prophecies, Ezekiel 11:17 states, "This is what the Sovereign LORD says: 'I will gather you from the nations and bring you back from the countries

How do you handle unexpected bad news? Do you respond stoically, refusing to show any emotion? Do you rely only on your own inner strength to weather life's storms? These were not Nehemiah's responses. Instead, he did two things: He allowed his emotions to react to the tragedy for a period of time, and he reached out to God in prayer for help. This twofold approach allowed Nehemiah to accept the tragedy and receive divine assistance in moving beyond it.

In Mark 9, Jesus was questioned by His disciples about why they could not cast a spirit out of a young man. Jesus responded by saying, "This kind can come forth by nothing, but by prayer and fasting" (v. 29, KJV). While not all manuscripts include the "*and fasting*," there is a principle here. Because of the seemingly impossible nature of the task (see also Mark 9:23), it called for a riveting focus upon the divine resource available. As the Bible presents fasting, it expresses one's true religious devotion and focus.

In 721 B.C. the Assyrians forced ten of the tribes of Israel to leave the land of Canaan, and in 586 B.C. the rest of the Israelites were exiled from the land by the Babylonians.

A cupbearer was an official of high rank among ancient Near Eastern kings. He acted as both an adviser and a bodyguard, ensuring that the king's drinks were safe for consumption. No doubt, the cupbearer had the confidence of the king in many matters and, therefore, influenced many of his decisions.

where you have been scattered, and I will give you back the land of Israel again.'"

In his prayer Nehemiah then confessed that God had indeed acted in behalf of His people and kept His promise. In a glorious display of His power, He had allowed the Jews to return to their homeland. This had happened in 538 B.C. under the rule of the Persian king Cyrus.

Nehemiah concluded his prayer by asking God to act in his behalf. Just as God had given Israel a special blessing from a former Persian king, so now Nehemiah asked God to help him obtain a special favor from Artaxerxes. Nehemiah was in a special position to make a request of the king because he was the royal cupbearer, one who helped to protect the king.

■ *Nehemiah's response at hearing of the condi-*
■ *tion at Jerusalem was to fast and pray, seek-*
■ *ing God's divine guidance.*

Nehemiah's Journey to Jerusalem (2:1–10)

In this section Nehemiah boldly acted on his faith as he asked the king for permission to take a leave of absence from his job and rebuild the walls of Jerusalem. By the grace of God, Artaxerxes granted Nehemiah's request.

Nehemiah's Request and Artaxerxes Response (2:1–8)

Approximately four months after Nehemiah received word of the Jews' problems in Jerusalem, Nehemiah violated the rules of courtly life in Susa by displaying an improper attitude in the king's presence. The look of sadness on his face put his life at risk, since it might be interpreted as displeasure with and thus rebellion against the king.

Artaxerxes took notice of Nehemiah's unacceptable facial expression. He concluded that his cupbearer was not physically ill and, therefore, must have an attitude problem of some sort—"Why is your face sad though you are not sick?" (v. 2, NASB). The words Artaxerxes' spoke in response to his observations struck fear in Nehemiah's heart. In all likelihood, Nehemiah must have wondered if he would be punished for treason.

To reassure his master and protect himself, Nehemiah responded first by expressing his loyalty to the Persian king. After wishing the king an infinitely long life, Nehemiah let Artaxerxes know the burden he had been carrying around for four months. Artaxerxes, who evidently considered Nehemiah more of a friend than an employee, asked his cupbearer what he would like to do to deal with the problem of Jerusalem's ruined condition.

The king's sincere question was an answer to Nehemiah's months of prayer for Jerusalem. He boldly asked the king for permission to take a leave of absence from his duties at Susa to rebuild Jerusalem. Understandably, the king and his wife were hesitant to give up Nehemiah's valuable services, not to mention his companionship, for a lengthy period of time. When asked how long he might be gone, Nehemiah responded with what seemed to be an acceptably short time to the king. Satisfied that Nehemiah would not be gone too long, Artaxerxes approved Nehemiah's plan. Furthermore, Nehemiah was also granted permission to have a military escort to travel the dangerous

Persian courtly etiquette prohibited people from displaying a negative emotion or being improperly dressed in the presence of the king. Failure to fulfill both of these conditions could be interpreted as dissatisfaction with the king. Thus, the king could impose the death penalty on anyone violating these rules. Mordecai, in Esther 4:2, was not permitted into the king's presence because he was wearing sackcloth. Here Nehemiah put his life at risk by wearing a sad expression before the king.

highways in Trans-Euphrates, the province which encompassed Judah.

After Nehemiah's trip had been approved, he dared to ask the king to fund the rebuilding of Jerusalem with resources from the Persian treasury. By God's grace, "the gracious hand of God was on me" (v. 8, NLT—a phrase also used several times within the book of Ezra), this brash request was also approved. Valuable timber resources from the government-controlled forests, perhaps those of Lebanon or Judah, would be delivered to Jerusalem.

Letter Delivery and Opposition (2:9–10)

With the king's approval of these tasks having been granted, letters were written to open up access for Nehemiah and the Jews to the valuable natural resources. At the same time, a sizable military guard was assembled to accompany Nehemiah on the eleven-hundred-mile journey back to his ancestral home.

Sanballat (Babylonian, "Sin {the moon god} has given life") was governor of Samaria. Tobiah (meaning "the LORD is gracious") was probably governor of the Persian-controlled Transjordan. No doubt, Nehemiah's coming was a threat to their authority over the area. As the king's personal advisor and cupbearer, he, if anyone, could fortify the city.

Among the officials around Jerusalem who were informed of Artaxerxes' decrees were Sanballat the Horonite and Tobiah the Ammonite. Both had much to lose if the Jews strengthened their hold on the city—the largest in the region. Thus, both were quite disturbed with the Persian king's decision.

■ *Nehemiah's burden over Jerusalem's condi-*
■ *tion became apparent to the king who in turn*
■ *permitted him to go to Jerusalem. Addition-*
■ *ally, provision was made for safe travel and*
■ *access to timbers for building needs.*

QUESTIONS TO GUIDE YOUR STUDY

1. Where was Nehemiah living when the book of Nehemiah opens?
2. What news from Jerusalem caused Nehemiah to be sad?
3. What did Nehemiah do about his sadness?
4. How did King Artaxerxes respond to Nehemiah's request?

NEHEMIAH'S INSPECTION OF THE WALLS (2:11–20)

Nehemiah and his military guard safely made the eleven-hundred-mile journey. Once there, Nehemiah took three days to assess Jerusalem's ruins. After presenting the challenge of rebuilding the city's wall, the officials agreed. However, enemies sought to destroy their efforts.

Secretive Night Inspection (2:11–16)

Nehemiah's first move was to take an initial, secret inspection by night of the city. He first toured the city, accompanied by some of his bodyguards. As the most important man in the group, Nehemiah rode on an animal—perhaps a mule or donkey (v. 12). Known only to Nehemiah at this time was the reason for the inspection.

Nehemiah's tour was a partial one, covering only the southern portions of Jerusalem. The tour of the walls was limited to this part of the city because nothing remained of the wall on the city's northern edge following the Babylonian destruction.

Nehemiah began his tour of the remaining portions of the wall by passing through the Valley Gate, probably a passageway located along Jerusalem's western wall overlooking the Tyropoeon Valley. Then he went in the direction of the Jackal Well ("dragon well," KJV), thought to be En Rogel (see Josh. 15:7–8; 2 Sam. 17:17). Passing beyond that, Nehemiah and those accompanying him went to the Dung Gate, probably the exit on the south side of the city that led most directly to the city dump located in the Hinnom Valley. From there Nehemiah went to the Fountain Gate and King's Pool (perhaps the Pool of Siloam), likely located on the southeastern side of the city. Some scholars speculate that the King's Pool had been constructed by King Hezekiah during the seventh century B.C. for the purpose of providing water for the area's impressive royal garden (see 2 Kings 25:4).

From this point Nehemiah apparently encountered a wall that had collapsed; thus, the animal upon which he was riding was unable to pass through it. As a result, Nehemiah had to inspect the wall from the bottom of the Kidron Valley, the low spot east of Jerusalem between the main city and the Mount of Olives.

Upon careful examination of what remained of Jerusalem's walls, Nehemiah retraced his steps along the southeastern, southern, and western perimeters. Then he reentered Jerusalem through the Valley Gate.

How do you respond to the challenge of doing God's work? Under Nehemiah's leadership, the Jews were ready and willing to begin the task of rebuilding Jerusalem's walls. Paul reminded us never to lack zeal in the service of God's work (see Rom. 12:11).

■ *Nehemiah secretly—at night and with only a*
■ *few men—inspected Jerusalem's city walls*
■ *and gates to evaluate their condition.*

Challenge and Opposition (2:17–20)

Upon completing the secret nighttime tour, Nehemiah met with the religious and political leaders of the city. He began by addressing the local officials, reminding them of the devastating condition of Jerusalem's walls. As a result the city was in a state of shame and disgrace. He then explained how God had inspired him to lead in rebuilding the wall and how God had led Artaxerxes to finance the task from the Persian treasury. Jerusalem's officials were impressed and encouraged by Nehemiah's words. They immediately extended their support toward the undertaking.

However, not everyone in the region shared Nehemiah's dream of rebuilding Jerusalem's defenses. Leading the opposition were Sanballat the Horonite, Tobiah the Ammonite, and Geshem the Arab. Sensing that Nehemiah's plans threatened their ability to control and intimidate the Jews living in the region, they accused Nehemiah of leading a rebellion against King Artaxerxes. Nehemiah's curt response was that they had no historic claim to the city and that the Jews were going to exercise their ancestral right to fortify their city. Confidently Nehemiah asserted, "The God of heaven will give us success" (v. 20).

Geshem (meaning "rain") the Arab was a man thought to have been a prominent leader of a confederacy of non-Jewish groups living in southern Palestine and the Sinai Desert region.

■ *When Nehemiah approached the city offi-*
■ *cials with the challenge of repairing the*
■ *walls, they enthusiastically agreed to do so;*
■ *however, enemies ridiculed them for their*
■ *desire, claiming they were rebellious.*

Nehemiah was committed to the task of rebuilding the wall, despite opposition. His commitment stemmed from his confidence in the Lord.

EFFORTS TO REBUILD THE WALL (3:1–32)

Nehemiah had initiated the task of rebuilding Jerusalem's walls, but completing the task would take the efforts of many others. This

The wall that was to be repaired was shaped like a long, slender, misshapen hourglass that was wide at the top (the north side) and narrow at the bottom (the south). The western and eastern sections of the wall were long and irregular.

In all likelihood, the northern section of the wall would have been the most heavily damaged, because it was located in the place most easily attacked. The towers would have been especially important for defensive purposes, since they would have provided those defending Jerusalem with the ability to observe approaching enemies from a great distance and the ability to fire weapons down on their nearby attackers.

section provides a detailed description of the Jewish families who joined with Nehemiah to repair the walls that had lain in ruins for 140 years. Nehemiah began at the city's northeast corner and continued counterclockwise around the wall.

Northern Section (3:1–5)

The description of the rebuilding efforts is an orderly one. Nehemiah began the work on the wall protecting the northern side of the city and then proceeded counterclockwise, to work on the western, southern, and eastern portions of the wall. For the purpose of working on the wall, it was subdivided into about forty-five sections, with the rebuilding task being shared by about forty work parties.

The first person mentioned as participating with Nehemiah in rebuilding the wall was Eliashib the high priest. He led a group of priests in the task of rebuilding the Sheep Gate, the Tower of the Hundred, the Tower of Hananel, and the walls connecting these features together. The priests were thus responsible for constructing most of the northern face of the city wall.

Working next to the priests on the western edge of the northern wall were men who had come from Jericho, a city located approximately fifteen miles east of Jerusalem. Next to them was a section built by Zaccur. The Fish Gate, rebuilt by the sons of Hassenaah, was probably located at the western corner of the north wall.

Reference is made in verse 5 to the Tekoites, those from Tekoa. Tekoa was about eleven miles from Jerusalem and was the hometown of the prophet Amos. The leaders from Tekoa refused to help with the project.

■ *Nehemiah began his efforts at reconstruction*
■ *with Jerusalem's northern walls and gates.*

The Western Section (3:6–13)

The western wall contained two gates and a tower. Rebuilding this vast stretch of the city's defenses required the help of many individuals. While scholars disagree as to the actual rendering of the latter part of verse 12, it is possible that women also helped in this endeavor.

The Jeshanah Gate (also known as the Old Gate) was repaired by Joiada. Several people are mentioned by name as playing a leading role in helping to rebuild the western wall. These individuals were likely responsible for enlisting crews to help them in the tasks. Many of these were leading citizens in the community: two were governors and at least two others were manufacturers of expensive commodities (note vv. 8–9, 12).

However, many Jews who did not live in Jerusalem also participated in this massive undertaking. Among the groups of volunteers who helped were those from Gibeon, Mizpah, and Zanoah. The group from Zanoah repaired 500 yards of the wall, in addition to the Valley Gate.

A main part of repairing Jerusalem's wall included rebuilding the city's gates. Chapter 3 mentions ten gates in all. Enemy assaults were usually heaviest at the gates.

■ *The western section of the wall was of con-*
■ *siderable length and, therefore, necessitated*
■ *the help of many. Among those who helped*
■ *were dignitaries and area Jews outside of*
■ *Jerusalem.*

The Southern and Eastern Sections (3:14–32)

The southern section of the wall was the shortest section and contained the Dung Gate (or Refuse Gate). Malkijah repaired this section. Verse 14 indicates he was the ruler of the district of Beth Hakkerem.

The eastern wall was longer than its western counterpart, measuring approximately fourteen hundred yards. It contained five gates and one large defensive tower. However, the Bible seems to indicate that only one of these gates required repair at this time—the Fountain Gate (see v. 15). Perhaps the eastern wall had received less damage during war than other portions of the wall. This would be likely since it was built upon the crest of a hill.

As with the western wall, work on the eastern wall was undertaken by many Jews. Regional Jewish leaders in the areas of politics, religion, and business assumed responsibility for assembling work crews to carry out the task. Rulers from Mizpah, Beth Zur, Keilah, and Mizpah—in addition to some leading priests, temple servants, and goldsmiths—are specifically mentioned as contributing to the project.

Emphasis is given to houses and other buildings in verses 15–32. Some people were apparently motivated to help with the wall by the desire to protect their personal property. Five individuals as well as a group of priests repaired the sections of the wall that were next to their private residences. Finally, groups of volunteers not associated with any named leader did their part as well. Among these were some men from Tekoa (who had also helped out on the wall's western side), some goldsmiths, and some merchants.

The gates and sections of Jerusalem's walls were not all in the same condition of disrepair. Second Kings 25:9 indicates Nebuchadnezzar destroyed that which was most important: "He destroyed all the important buildings in the city" (NLT). In doing so, the city could be crippled at its most crucial points.

Some scholars suggest that the difference in style between 3:1–15 and 3:16–32 is because these were originally two different lists. However, it seems reasonable to conclude that the emphasis upon houses in the latter passage is a description of efforts to protect personal property.

- *While the wall's southern section seemingly*
- *included one individual to oversee its repair,*
- *the eastern section included many individu-*
- *als, including those who sought to defend*
- *their personal property.*

OPPOSITION TO REBUILDING THE WALL (4:1–23)

Again the efforts of Nehemiah are met with ridicule by Sanballat, Tobiah, and others. Although the enemies make efforts to fight against Jerusalem, the Jews took their discouragement to God and guarded the city. Work efforts continued under the diligent and capable leadership of Nehemiah.

The Work Ridiculed (4:1–8)

Organized opposition to the Jews increased when it became clear that they would carry out their intentions to rebuild Jerusalem's defenses. No one was more troubled by the Jews' progress than Sanballat, the governor of the nearby territory of Samaria. He at first expressed his anger toward the Jews by ridiculing them, hoping to humiliate them and, thus, discourage them. Calling them feeble, he asked a series of questions in an effort to undermine their confidence and progression. Tobiah the Ammonite joined in the ridicule, suggesting that the weight of even a small animal—a fox—walking on the wall would cause it to fall.

Nehemiah responded to the insults of Sanballat and Tobiah by praying to God rather than lashing out against the detractors. Nehemiah left revenge to God, asking Him to pay back the

In verse 5 Nehemiah requests that God not forgive the sins of the enemies. This is reminiscent of the imprecatory psalms—those calling for the destruction of Israel's enemies. Note, for example, Psalms 69:22–25 and 109:6–15.

As we do God's will, Satan often threatens us by diverting our focus on the obstacles that stand in the way. Nehemiah did not spend time responding to the enemies' threats. His focus was on finishing the wall. Where does your "focus" lie when obstacles threaten God's work?

enemies accordingly for the wrongs they had committed (note vv. 4–5).

Nehemiah and the rest of the Jews wisely invested their efforts in the task of rebuilding the wall instead of responding to their enemies. Before long, all the gaps in the wall were closed; and, due to the peoples' concerted efforts, the wall reached half its height. This progress alarmed the enemies, and a large group of them decided to destroy the work before it could be completed. Sanballat, Tobiah, the Arabs, the Ammonites, and certain residents of Ashdod (a former Philistine town converted to a district capital under Persian control) devised a strategy to attack Jerusalem and cause further harassment.

- *Though Sanballat harassed the Jews, they*
- *diligently continued making progress in*
- *their work until he further threatened to*
- *attack them for their efforts.*

Discouragement and Fear (4:9–14)

Sanballat's added threat did not stop the Jews. Instead, it drove them closer to God and made them more careful. From this point on until the wall was completed, the Jews assigned some of their men the task of providing around-the-clock armed-guard duty for the city.

The added stress caused by the opposition, combined with the grind of backbreaking labor everyday from dawn till dusk, began to overwhelm the Jewish laborers. Jews living near the opposition repeatedly warned the workers of the seriousness of the threats, and in response even more guards were posted. Each guard was armed with swords, spears, and bows—weapons designed for both long-range and close combat. Meanwhile, Nehemiah inspired the troops by appealing to their faith in God and their desire to protect their families (note v. 14).

- *The Jews, though discouraged and weary in*
- *their task, were reminded by Nehemiah that*
- *God is great and awesome and that they*
- *should fight for their families.*

Resurgence to Continue (4:15–23)

Nehemiah's strategic use of heavily armed guards around the work site forced the opposition to abandon their original plan of attack on Jerusalem. In order to keep them away from the wall, Nehemiah permanently assigned 50 percent of the work force to active military duty and provided them with both weapons and armor. And because of the seriousness of the threat of violence against the Jews, Nehemiah made all of the men involved in carrying materials and actually doing the building also carry weapons with them (see vv. 17–18).

Additionally, Nehemiah established an emergency response procedure in the event of an attack. At the sound of the trumpet, all workers would immediately assemble for battle there. Nehemiah reminded the Jews that God would fight for them. Moreover, no one involved in the project would be permitted to leave Jerusalem, even to go home at night. The men would now be required to do nightwatch duty, in addition to their daytime labors. So demanding was the routine that no one even took the time to

Paul reminds us in the book of Galatians to continue in that which is worthwhile. "So don't get tired of doing what is good. Don't get discouraged and give up, for we will reap a harvest of blessing at the appropriate time" (6:9, NLT). Though penned long after Nehemiah's time, he knew the importance of perseverance. When the stresses mount, do you "give up" or "keep at it"? See also Hebrews 12:11.

change their clothes. They remained fully clothed and armed at all times, even while performing the most menial of tasks (note v. 23).

- *Nehemiah's strategic plan allowed the Jews*
- *to continue their labors while also being*
- *thoroughly prepared for defense in the event*
- *of a military attack.*

PROBLEMS WITHIN THE COMMUNITY (5:1–19)

The threats the Jews faced at this time were not only from outsiders. Some of the most serious troubles they faced came from the forces of nature and other Jews. The task of rebuilding the walls was undertaken during a time of famine, and some of the Jews had abused their brothers by selling them as slaves. Nehemiah called for this usury to stop. Moreover, he denied himself the prerogative of receiving taxes as governor in order to help the people.

Abuse of the Poor (5:1–5)

The food supply during this time period was scarce and money to buy it even more so. The added stress of finishing the wall under the duress of enemy threats drove the already oppressed, poorer Jews to the point of rebellion.

Men and women alike came together in revolt. They brought four serious issues to Nehemiah's attention. First, the people lacked food. Many did not even have enough grain to feed their children. Second, in order to purchase food the people were forced to mortgage their houses, fields, and vineyards. Third, the taxes imposed by the Persian government on all the landowners had forced the people to borrow money to pay their taxes to the government. Finally, to raise the money to pay their debts, many had been forced to sell their sons and daughters into slavery to other Jews.

- *Many of the Jews protested against the*
- *wealthier Jews because of the economic con-*
- *dition of the area. The sad state of affairs had*
- *resulted in family members being sold as*
- *slaves.*

Nehemiah's Response (5:6–13)

Nehemiah was justifiably outraged at what he heard; however, he took some time to think things over and then met with the businessmen and politicians responsible for the added hardships. He accused these men of violating a basic economic law found in the Law of Moses. They were charging fellow Jews interest on loans. In a large public meeting, Nehemiah forced both sides of the problem to come together. Nehemiah rebuked the wealthy Jewish oppressors for their socially destructive practices that were based on greed. Particularly troubling was the practice of taking the Jews given to them in exchange for loans, and then selling these as slaves to non-Jews, who in turn sold them back to the Jews at a considerable profit. The Law of Moses prohibited such sales (see Exod. 21:8). Verse 6 points out that these actions were wrong; furthermore, these men should have let their reverence for God and His Law guide their actions. Nehemiah and many others were lending people money and providing them with grain, but in ways that did not offend God.

Persian kings were notorious for depleting the monetary wealth from the nations they ruled. Historians estimate that about 20 million darics—Persian gold coins worth about four days' wages each—were collected in taxes per year by the Persian government, with much of the coinage being melted down into bars of gold and silver and kept in Susa. Alexander the Great conquered Susa and is said to have discovered about 340 tons of gold and more than 1,500 tons of silver there.

Deuteronomy 23:19–20 indicates that God's blessing would result if the Jews did not charge their fellow Jews interest when lending money, food, or anything else. See also Exodus 22:25 and Leviticus 25:36.

65

Using his Persian authority, Nehemiah ordered the greedy Jewish business leaders to stop their usury and to return the property they had taken. The businessmen pledged to change their ways. To ensure they would carry out their promise, Nehemiah made the men take a solemn oath before the Lord to bind them to the terms of their agreement. He also placed a curse on the wealth of anyone who broke his word, symbolized by the "shaking out" of the folds of his robe (note v. 13). The people who had witnessed these proceedings voiced their approval and joyously praised the Lord.

- *Nehemiah met with those who were guilty of*
- *abusing their fellow Jews and pointed them*
- *to their violation of the Law of Moses. In a*
- *public meeting they pledged to give back*
- *everything and demand nothing more from*
- *the people.*

Nehemiah's Worthy Leadership Example (5:14–19)

Nehemiah interrupted his account of rebuilding the wall to discuss further efforts he had made at making conditions more tolerable for the Jewish citizens of the region. During his first term as governor of the district of Judah, a period of twelve years extending from 444–432 B.C., Nehemiah did not make the people provide food supplies for the administrative center. Also, he apparently did not require the people to pay an additional tax to support the local government office. Nehemiah's behavior contrasted sharply with that of the previous Jewish governors. They had required the commoners to supply their households (and other administrators') with food and wine, but they also forced people to hand over forty shekels—about a pound—of silver for the benefit of the governor as well. Nehemiah did none of this because of His reverence for God. As a God-fearing political leader, he focused only on what would benefit his community most: completing Jerusalem's wall.

As a Persian governor Nehemiah was required to entertain and provide meals for many people. It was customary for governors to obtain the food served at these banquets from the citizens over whom they administered. Nehemiah indicated that each day he usually had more than one hundred fifty people eating at his table. Not surprisingly, large amounts of meat were required for these meals each day: one ox, six sheep, and several chickens. Rather than take these from the local farmers' herds and flocks, he took them from his own possessions instead, in order not to place an even heavier burden on the people.

- *Nehemiah did not use his position as governor to gain wealth or favor from others. He sought to help his fellow Jews and looked to God for his reward.*

FURTHER ENEMY OPPOSITION (6:1–19)

This section resumes the narrative account of rebuilding the wall following the interlude of 5:14–19. Sanballat and the enemies plotted to thwart Nehemiah's efforts, this time by killing him. Though several attempts were made to pull Nehemiah away from the project and discourage him, he never gave in. Thus, the wall was completed.

Though Nehemiah was in a position of power, he did not use it as a means to manipulate or take advantage of others. He was willing, rather, to use his position to serve the people. What leadership positions do you hold? Do you use them to get or to give?

Nehemiah's mention of poultry here marks the first mention of chickens in the Bible. Chickens were first domesticated in the Indus River valley around 2000 B.C. and were known to have been in Egypt no later than the fifteenth century B.C. The earliest indisputable evidence of chickens in Israel comes from an Israelite seal dated ca. 600 B.C. which had a rooster engraved on it.

Plot of the Enemies (6:1–9)

Although at this point Jerusalem's wall had been repaired, there were still several openings in the structure because the doors had not yet been set in place. Becoming increasingly desperate, Sanballat, Tobiah, and Geshem renewed their efforts to shut down the project before it could be completed. They proposed that a regional conference be held on the plain of Ono. However, Nehemiah took their invitation for what it really was, a plot to kill him. Therefore, he declined the request, indicating he could not take time away from his responsibilities in Jerusalem. Though they asked him repeatedly, four times in all, he consistently turned them down. In spite of their persistent efforts, Nehemiah stayed focused on the work at hand.

Ono was in Israelite territory west of Jerusalem (not far from modern Tel Aviv) and was probably a site considered to be neutral.

When that strategy failed, Sanballat became more intimidating. He sent an unsealed letter to Nehemiah suggesting that rumors were floating around to the effect that the Jews were planning to mount a rebellion against Artaxerxes, with Nehemiah himself positioning himself as a mutinous king. Moreover, Sanballat threatened to pass these rumors along to Artaxerxes if Nehemiah did not leave Jerusalem to meet with Sanballat. By leaving the letter unsealed, he put further pressure on Nehemiah by leaving open the possibility that these damaging charges had been read—and consequently spread—by many others. He hoped the Jews would be so afraid of Persian military intervention that they would give up their work on the wall.

Admirably, Nehemiah did not let Sanballat's latest efforts turn him aside from his task. Armed with the truth, Nehemiah branded the latest charges as imaginative lies created by Sanballat himself. Then he prayed for strength to handle the added stress caused by his enemies' persistent efforts.

Nehemiah was a man of prayer. He knew the importance and value of seeking God's help in troubled times. We, too, have divine resources for life's crucial issues. Are you a person of prayer?

■ *As the Jews neared the completion of their*
■ *project, their enemies became increasingly*
■ *desperate. They plotted to draw Nehemiah*
■ *outside Jerusalem and kill him, and they*
■ *spread vicious false rumors.*

The Use of Intimidation (6:10–14)

Sanballat had some allies among the Jews. One key Jewish opponent to Nehemiah was Shemaiah, an individual who was apparently both a priest and a prophet. In what may have been a symbolic action on the part of the prophet, Shemaiah confined himself to his house. When Nehemiah visited him there, Shemaiah suggested that they seek refuge from those who wanted to kill him by locking themselves inside the Temple, living as virtual prisoners there. However, such a move on Nehemiah's part would have disrupted his task of overseeing the rebuilding project and dishonored him by making him act as a coward or criminal.

In Old Testament Law the altar in the central place of worship was recognized as a place where people who feared for their lives could go for refuge (see Exod. 21:13–14). During the days of King Solomon both Adonijah and Joab took hold of the corners of the altar (the "horns") in order to try to seek pardon and protection for their lives (see 1 Kings 1:50; 2:28).

Nehemiah concluded that though Shemaiah was a prophet he was not speaking by the inspiration of God. He had been hired by Sanballat and Tobiah to intimidate and discredit Nehemiah. Having unmasked the plan, Nehemiah made no effort to arrest or destroy Shemaiah. Instead, he left vengeance in God's hands. Nehemiah asked God to bring judgment on the individuals, Jews and non-Jews alike, who had tried to shut down his efforts to lead. In his petition to God, Nehemiah revealed that numerous false prophets, including the prophetess Noadiah, had all attempted to intimidate him by issuing warnings in God's name.

■ *Jewish false prophets cooperated with*
■ *non-Jewish opponents to the wall. Though*
■ *they tried to intimidate Nehemiah and get*
■ *him to give up the project, he did not give up.*

Completion of the Wall (6:15–16)

Miraculously, the basic defensive wall around Jerusalem, one that had lain in ruins for more than 140 years, was rebuilt in only fifty-two days. It was completed on the twenty-fifth of Elul, a date usually understood to correspond to October 2, 445 B.C.

It was an incredible accomplishment that the wall around Jerusalem was rebuilt in only fifty-two days. Paul reminds us in Ephesians 3:20 that God "is able to do exceeding abundantly beyond all that we ask or think" (NASB).

This incredible feat, accomplished in spite of the multitude of threats and plots mounted against the builders, served as a major defeat for its opponents. Jews and non-Jews alike who had tried to stop the rebuilding recognized that this project was completed with God's help. This truth was particularly troubling for the detractors who were Jews because it meant that they had been opposing their own God.

■ *With God's help, the Jews rebuilt the*
■ *long-ruined wall in only fifty-two days.*

Tobiah's Efforts at Opposition (6:17–19)

Besides religious opposition from the Jews, Nehemiah had also faced opposition from many of his own nobles. These individuals had business contracts with Tobiah requiring them to be loyal to him; Tobiah had forced them to act as both messengers and informants regarding Nehemiah's activities.

- Nehemiah's efforts to rebuild the wall had
- also been opposed by many Jewish leaders.

QUESTIONS TO GUIDE YOUR STUDY

1. What was Nehemiah's first task when he came to Jerusalem?
2. Describe Nehemiah's strategy for rebuilding the wall.
3. What opposition did Nehemiah experience in rebuilding the wall?
4. How did Nehemiah respond both to external threats and internal problems?

LIST OF FIRST EXILE RETURNEES (7:1–73)

Now that Jerusalem's wall had been completed, new challenges arose. To benefit from the defenses, people were needed to guard the gates, and a larger population was needed within the city. Before instituting his plan to increase the city's population, Nehemiah did some research; he began by locating a list of exiles who had returned to Jerusalem in 538 B.C.

Provision for Jerusalem's Protection (7:1–3)

Nehemiah wanted to do more than simply restore the walls and gates of Jerusalem; he sought to revitalize other aspects of the life of the city. To make sure that the defensive advantages provided by the wall would be utilized, he appointed persons to secure the gates, the most vulnerable parts of the wall. To enhance the worship of God within the city, he appointed singers and Levites to perform duties at the Jerusalem Temple. To fortify the political and military aspects of the city, Nehemiah appointed two trusted and godly leaders to oversee these vital areas of the city's life. He appointed his brother Hanani as governor and Hananiah as commander of the military forces in Jerusalem.

Not only did Nehemiah appoint gatekeepers to take charge of the passageways through the wall, but he also established strict rules about when the gates could be opened. To minimize the risk of attack on the city, the gates could only be opened well after sunrise and must be securely closed before sundown. Furthermore, Jerusalem's residents would be required to perform guard duty for the city, usually on the wall in front of their houses.

■ *To help Jerusalem benefit from its new wall,*
■ *Nehemiah made provision for the gates and*
■ *walls to be guarded.*

Nehemiah's Discovery of Genealogical Records (7:4–73)

With the wall now completed, it was necessary to make provisions for the interior of the holy city to be repaired and populated. In preparation for these tasks Nehemiah made use of some official census records to help determine who should live in Jerusalem.

List of Returnees (7:4–65)

At this point two other problems needed to be addressed in Jerusalem: there was a disproportionately small population of Jews living in the newly protected city, and there was not enough decent housing for new residents. To address these issues, especially the first problem,

Nehemiah called together all the Jews of the region for the purpose of taking a census. The data he obtained was used to redistribute the Jewish population in the region.

One of the purposes of the census was to determine the families who could verify their status as full-blooded Jews. To help in determining the Jewish identity of the people in the area, Nehemiah made use of a census list closely related to the one found in Ezra 2. The list found in Nehemiah omits the city name Magbish along with its number of inhabitants, uses four different names for individuals or cities (Binnui for Bani, Hariph for Jorah, Gibeon for Gibbar, and Beth Azmaveth for Azmaveth), has different figures for nineteen names on the list, and when added together the figures in Nehemiah 7:8–62 are 1,271 higher than the corresponding figures in Ezra 2:3–60.

Except for minor differences, the lists in Ezra 2 and Nehemiah 7 are identical. The differences are mainly in the spelling of names and probably arose in the course of the transmission of the text.

■ *As a first step toward increasing Jerusalem's*
■ *population and repairing its ruined build-*
■ *ings, Nehemiah assembled the people and*
■ *had them register in a census.*

Totals (7:66–73)

The difference between the sum of the totals listed in verses 8–62 (31,089) and the total derived from verses 66–67 (49,942) is sizable (18,808). Some people propose that the larger number includes women and children, that it includes priests who are otherwise not counted, or that it includes members of the northern tribes of Israel who had returned with people from Judah, Benjamin, and Levi.

Indications of the general economic level of those who returned initially to Jerusalem are seen in the numbers of animals the Jews brought with them. There was approximately one animal for every five persons in the group—perhaps about one per family.

Nehemiah and Ezra also have different totals for the amount of precious metals and priestly clothing donated to the Temple treasury by various wealthy Jews. According to Ezra 61,000 drachmas of gold were given (about 1,045 lbs.), though Nehemiah mentions only 41,000 drachmas (about 670 lbs.). Ezra states the silver totaled 5,000 minas (about 6,250 lbs.), whereas Nehemiah lists it as 4,200 (about 5,250 lbs.). Nehemiah mentions 597 priestly garments, while Ezra mentions only 100. As in the other discrepancies, the Bible is trustworthy in its account. Many scholars explain these discrepancies as lists from two different times or examples of errors introduced by copyists.

- *In connection with the registration of citi-*
- *zens in Judah, Nehemiah made use of a cen-*
- *sus list closely related to the one found in*
- *Ezra 2.*

REVIVAL AMONG THE PEOPLE (8:1–9:38)

Shortly after his journey to Jerusalem, Ezra led the Jews in a great revival. The revival began with the public reading of God's Word and the observance of a great religious festival. It resulted in confession of sins and the worship of God.

Ezra's Reading of the Law (8:1–12)

On the first day of the seventh month of the Jewish religious calendar year (Tishri, September-October), Ezra called the people together for a time of the public reading of the Law of Moses. The meeting occurred in 445 B.C. and seems to have come about as a result of the peoples' revitalized spiritual interest following the successful completion of the wall.

This all-important public meeting took place in the open area just inside the Water Gate, located on the eastern side of Jerusalem. For this event Ezra invited adult men and women, as well as all the younger people who were able to understand. The central event in this meeting consisted of Ezra reading the Book of the Law for about five hours (from daybreak until noon) to the assembled group. Disagreement exists as to exactly what was contained in the scroll Ezra read. It could have been the entire Law of Moses (all of Genesis–Deuteronomy) or merely a selection of laws taken from these books.

For this special event Ezra ordered the construction of a large wooden platform that allowed him to stand above the crowd. A total of fourteen men—Ezra and thirteen others—stood on the platform throughout the reading of the Law. As a show of respect for God's Word, everyone in the crowd stood up when they saw that Ezra was opening the holy scroll.

Before beginning the reading, Ezra took time to give praise to God. The people expressed their wholehearted agreement with Ezra's words by raising their hands, shouting "Amen," and then bowing deeply with their faces to the ground to show reverence for God.

Worship only occurs as we are ready to "receive" or "hear" from God. The verbal and visual expression of praise evidenced from the assembly before Ezra's reading gives evidence of the peoples' readiness. What do you do in preparation to hear from God? What should you be doing?

Thirteen Levites, members of the tribe assigned to lead Israel in the worship of God, assisted their fellow-tribesman Ezra in the task of instructing the people in the Word of God. Scattered among the people in the crowd, these men also read from the Law and then explained it so that the people would understand it more fully.

As the people heard the Word of God being read and explained to them, it affected them deeply, and many began to weep. But Nehemiah, Ezra, and the Levites encouraged the Israelites not to do so. The day was a holy one, and, therefore, should result in joy. Consequently, the Jewish leaders urged their fellow citizens to celebrate with the best of food and drink and to share their food freely. As Nehemiah noted, the real strength of their nation lay in their relationship with God, "for the joy of the LORD is your strength" (v. 10).

Encouraged by their leaders' words, the people left the public assembly for a time of grateful celebration and feasting. As a result of the day's remarkable assembly, many Jews had come to know and understand key truths about God for the first time in their lives.

- *At a great public meeting in the early fall,*
- *Ezra, assisted by the Levites and Nehemiah,*
- *read and explained the Law of God to the*
- *Jews. The people were deeply moved by what*
- *they heard.*

Celebration with the Feast of Tabernacles (8:13–18)

The next day, a smaller group composed of priests, Levites, and all the heads of Jewish families met with Ezra to receive additional instruction in the Law. Through their study, apparently of Leviticus 23:33–44, they learned that God required His covenant people to celebrate the Feast of Booths/Tabernacles during the seventh month (Tishri, September-October). For a week all Jews were to live in simple huts constructed of branches cut from trees that grew in the region.

The leaders ordered their people to keep the celebration, beginning on the fifteenth day of the month. The entire Jewish community in and around Jerusalem did as they had been instructed. On their flat rooftops and in their courtyards, including the Temple courtyard and near some city gates, they built small booths from branches. Each night for a week the families camped out in these simple structures as a means of remembering their origins and what God had done for them.

The community participated in the event so completely that it was the best-kept Feast of Booths since the days of Joshua almost a thousand years earlier (see v. 17). There was great joy in the community during that time.

During the weeklong celebration Ezra read the Book of the Law publicly during the daytime. The celebration was climaxed with a large public assembly.

■ *The spiritually revived Jews celebrated the*
■ *weeklong Feast of Tabernacles. During the*
■ *celebration they continued their study of*
■ *God's Word under Ezra.*

Preparation for Confession (9:1–3)

Ezra's public reading of the Word of God, in combination with the people's obedience to the festival requirements, had a significant impact on the Jewish community. Revival broke out among the people, and their desire to know more of God's Word increased.

After the activities associated with the Feast of Booths, the Jews gathered once again in Jerusalem for a solemn religious assembly. For the event the people denied themselves food, wore sackcloth, and threw dust on their heads—all signs of deep spiritual distress. At various points throughout the day, they participated in different activities: public confession of their sins and those of their forefathers, three hours of listening to the public reading of God's Word, and an additional three hours of confession of sins mixed with worship and praise of the Lord.

■ *The Jews expressed their renewed commit-*
■ *ment to God by expressing regret for their*
■ *sins, studying God's Word, and worshiping*
■ *Him.*

Confession and Worship (9:4–38)

Levites led the Israelites in the activities of confession and prayer and praise and worship. A powerful example of the Levites' praises offered to God is found in verses 5–37. The progression of topics here closely parallels those found in the Law of Moses and the presentation of Israelite history found in Joshua–2 Kings. Additionally, this poetic passage echoes thoughts found in some of the praise, nature, and historical psalms (cp. Pss. 8, 78, 104). Within these verses

Sackcloth was a garment of dark, coarsely woven goat or camel hair. It was generally worn as a sign of mourning and grief and, thus, characterized somber occasions. Its rough texture served as a means toward chastisement among the penitent.

God's glorious handiwork in nature and history are recounted.

In verses 5–6, God is praised as the highest and greatest being in the universe. He is acclaimed as the Maker of all—heaven and earth, along with everything in them. And He is praised by all the heavenly beings.

Besides being Lord of nature, God is seen as the shaper of Israelite history. God began His work in behalf of Israel with Abram, a Mesopotamian who proved faithful and trustworthy in his relationship with God. Graciously, God made a covenant with him, promising to give his descendants the land of Canaan.

God began to fulfill His bright promise when Israelite history was at its darkest. At the time when Israel suffered greatly as slaves in Egypt, God intervened through the forces of nature and set His people free. He provided leadership for them in the desert, bringing them to Mount Sinai where He gave them the gift of divine Law. Additionally, God also provided them food and water. Such provisions helped Israel emotionally, socially, spiritually, and physically.

In spite of these divine gifts, Israel ignored them and rejected God's good plan. Nevertheless, because of God's amazing forgiveness, patience, and compassion, He did not give up on the Israelites. Instead, He continued to teach them and provide for them throughout their entire forty-year period in the wilderness. He even provided Israel with additional land beyond what He had originally promised, giving them the territories of Sihon and Og east of the Jordan River.

God always meets the needs of His people (note Phil. 4:19). In fulfilling His promise to the Israelites, God met their needs in spite of Egyptian enslavement and wilderness wanderings. We may be assured that whatever our needs, God will supply them.

Summarizing events from the book of Joshua, the Levites noted that God kept His good promise to give Abraham's descendants the land of Canaan. God had led Israel in conquering the Canaanites, and their resources became the Israelites' to use and enjoy.

Unfortunately, these wonderful gifts from God were not enough to keep Israel loyal to Him. Once planted firmly in the Promised Land, Israel rejected God's divine law and turned away from Him. As a result, God had to fulfill one of His warnings, bringing conquering enemies against Israel. Yet when the nation finally cried out to Him for help, He raised up a rescuer to lead them to victory and renewed freedom. This pattern repeated itself, especially throughout the period of the judges.

To try to break this pattern, God sent prophets to the Israelites, warning them to submit again to God's Law. Unfortunately, the people continued in their stubborn, wicked ways and suffered the consequences; they were repeatedly handed over to their enemies. Amazingly, however, in spite of their disobedience the Israelites remained embraced by God's love.

Having recounted numerous examples of God's lavish love for His sinful people, the Levites now brought their review of Israelite history up to their own day. It was true that over the past three hundred years—since the days of Assyrian domination of Israel in 721 B.C. until the present—many of Israel's political, religious, and familial leaders had rejected God, and He had given Israel punishments the nation had deserved. Even Jews of their own generation had sinned against God and were experiencing a measure of God's judgment. For them it took the form of an oppressive economic burden placed on them by the Persians, who forced the Jews to pay heavy taxes.

■ *In the longest prayer of the book of*
■ *Nehemiah, Judah's leaders give praise to God*
■ *for His help to Israel in the past and confess*
■ *the sins of their forefathers and their own*
■ *sins.*

THE COVENANT AGREEMENT (10:1–39)

The psalmlike prayer of the Levites comes at this point to a climactic conclusion. Here the Jews pledged themselves to return wholeheartedly to God and to obey every detail of His Law. At the same time they asked the awesome God of Israel's past to exercise His lordship now by demonstrating His interest in Israel's present.

List of Those Who Signed the Covenant (10:1–27)

The pledge took the form of a written document which was signed by eighty-four of the religious and political leaders of the Jewish community in Judah. First to sign the official document was Nehemiah, the chief political officer in the region. Following him were twenty-two priests, seventeen Levites, and forty-four additional leaders of the people.

■ *Beginning with Nehemiah, the leading polit-*
■ *ical and religious leaders of the Jews sol-*
■ *emnly committed themselves to following*
■ *God's Law.*

Stipulations of the Covenant (10:28–39)

The covenant signed by the Jewish leaders required basic changes that would touch the daily lives of the Jews in the areas of marriage (forbidding marriage with non-Jews), weekly scheduling (keeping the Sabbath), and finances (payment of religious taxes and giving required offerings).

Pledge to Follow God's Laws (10:28–31)

Though only people in high-profile positions within the public life of Judah actually signed the document, all the other Jews who committed themselves to the Lord in the recent religious revival also bound themselves to the terms of the agreement. In fact, they took an oath of obedience to God's Law and placed themselves under a curse if they should ever violate the agreement. Among the people who took this pledge were whole households of additional priests, Levites, gatekeepers, singers, and Temple servants.

Verses 30–39 spell out key terms of the solemn covenant made between the Jews and God. First on the list was the commitment to maintain the racial purity of the covenant community. None of the heads of Jewish households would arrange marriages between their family members and non-Jews. The Law of Moses required this (see Exod. 34:15–16 and Deut. 7:1–4) in order to help the group avoid bringing pagan influences into the community of faith.

The people also committed themselves to observing Sabbath (see Exod. 20:10; Lev. 23:3; and Deut. 5:14) and sabbatical year regulations (see Exod. 23:10–11; Lev. 25:4–5; and Deut. 15:1–2) found in the Law of Moses, even when doing so meant financial loss.

The longest of the Ten Commandments dealt with the Sabbath (see Exod. 20:8–11). The Israelites regularly abused it throughout their history (see Jer. 17:21–23; Ezek. 22:8; and Amos 8:5).

Marriages in ancient Israel were not based on romance. Instead, the head of a family would determine whom his children would marry. Decisions about marriage were usually based on concerns for increasing the family's prestige, position, and wealth in the community; religious and relational considerations might also come into play, as is seen in Genesis 24:3–4 and Nehemiah 10:30.

Temple Taxes (10:32–33)

An additional commitment helped to provide financial support for the Temple in Jerusalem. Each year every adult male was to give one-third of a shekel (about one-eighth of an ounce) of silver to the Temple treasury. This money would be used to acquire sufficient grain and meat for the required daily rituals, the annual festivals, and the regular and special sacrifices made to God.

Offerings (10:34–39)

The priests and Levites accepted a special obligation as part of this agreement. They agreed to provide all the wood needed to maintain a perpetual altar fire that would be used to burn the animal and grain sacrifices made at the Temple (see Lev. 6:12). Earlier in Israelite history the non-Israelite Gibeonites had been forced to perform this duty (see Josh. 9:27).

Additionally, the people promised to bring food gifts to God that would be used for the benefit of the workers at the Temple (see Num. 18:9–14, 18–19). The firstfruits of all the crops and trees were to be brought to Jerusalem each year (see Exod. 23:19; 34:26), as were the first male offspring from each animal in the herd (see Exod. 13:2, 12–13). Even the firstborn male heir in the family was to be given to God, though the child was to be bought back by the family (Num. 18:15–16). On top of all this, one-tenth of all field, tree, and vine crops was to be given as gifts to God as well (see Gen. 14:20; Lev. 27:32).

The food gifts were to be set aside by the Levites in Temple storerooms. One-tenth of the produce collected by the Levites was then to be given over to the high priest.

The covenant agreement signed by the Jews called for the men to give less than what the Law of Moses required (a half-shekel; see Exod. 30:13). This probably reflected the degree of poverty the people experienced in post-exilic Israel.

■ *Following their leaders, all the Jews agreed*
■ *to follow God's laws, especially ones forbid-*
■ *ding interracial marriage and keeping the*
■ *Sabbath. They also pledged to support the*
■ *work of God at the Temple by paying an*
■ *annual tax and bringing in regular offerings.*

RESETTLEMENT DISTRIBUTION (11:1–36)

Jerusalem's defenses were now rebuilt, and work was being done to revitalize the city's life, especially at its worship center. Not only could the city now support a larger population, but it also needed one to sustain its vigor. The problem was, all of the Jews in the region had already settled down in private residences in the villages surrounding Jerusalem. To remedy the situation, Nehemiah took steps to increase the city's population.

Resettlement of Jerusalem (11:1–19)

To fill the newly fortified city with sufficient numbers of residents, Nehemiah required representatives from each of the major political and religious families to resettle in Jerusalem.

Family Heads (11:1–9)

Nehemiah required all the Jews of the region to cast lots—that is, to make a random selection of one-tenth of their total population to move into the walled city. A few individuals actually volunteered to move to Jerusalem. These people received special commendations for their decision.

In addition to the volunteers, individuals from the tribes of Judah, Benjamin, and Levi were also mentioned by Nehemiah as ones who relocated to Jerusalem. The list of new residents in Nehemiah is similar to, but not identical to, one found in 1 Chronicles 9:2–21. Scholars are not sure why the lists are different; perhaps they represent censuses taken at different times.

The listing in 1 Chronicles is more detailed than the one contained in Nehemiah. It also contains the names of different individuals and family lines and has higher figures than those found here.

The two most prominent members of the tribe of Judah that relocated to Jerusalem are Athaiah and Maaseiah. Nehemiah indicates that a total of 468 Judahites resettled in the city; 1 Chronicles 9:6 provides the figure 690.

Members of the tribe of Benjamin settled in Jerusalem in greater numbers than did the Judahites. Five Benjamite leaders moved there, creating a total of 928 men who came from that Israelite tribe. According to 1 Chronicles 9:9, 956 Benjamites relocated to Jerusalem.

Priests (11:10–14)

Six leaders among the priestly families—Jedaiah, the son of Joiarib, Jakin, Seraiah, Adaiah, and Amashsai—led the way in the priests' repopulation of Jerusalem during the days of Nehemiah. Nehemiah indicates that a total of 1,192 priests came to Jerusalem as part of this population shift; this total is smaller than the total of 1,760 found in 1 Chronicles 9:13.

Levites and Gatekeepers (11:15–19)

Nehemiah also listed six leaders who led non-priestly members of the tribe of Levi back into Jerusalem. These were Shemaiah, Shabbethai, Jozabad, Mattaniah, Bakbukiah, and Abda.

Additionally, Nehemiah engineered the move of 172 gatekeepers into the holy city. Their function was to watch over the ten gates that were part of the wall of Jerusalem.

- *In addition to volunteers who moved from*
- *surrounding villages to Jerusalem,*
- *Nehemiah required representatives from*
- *each of the major political and religious fam-*
- *ilies to resettle in Jerusalem.*

Resettlement of Judah and Benjamin (11:20–36)

Apparently the Temple servants were not required by Nehemiah to move within Jerusalem's city walls. They lived on Ophel, the hill nearest to the Temple outside the city wall.

The remaining 90 percent of the Jews continued to reside on their family estates in the towns and villages that had been part of the preexilic tribal territories of Judah and Benjamin. Among the individuals who played an important role in the life of Jerusalem, but who were not required to move within the city walls, were the Temple servants.

The chief officer of the Levites who oversaw their work in Jerusalem was Uzzi, a descendant of Asaph, the famous psalmist responsible for twelve of the Bible's psalms. As an indicator of the control of the Persian government in Jewish affairs, the Temple singers in Jerusalem had their activities regulated by King Artaxerxes.

During Nehemiah's time Jews were living in seventeen main villages in the territory that was originally given to the tribe of Judah. The settlements were located south of Jerusalem in a thirty-two-mile-wide band that extended from Beersheba to the Valley of Hinnom just outside of Jerusalem. This relatively small number of locations is far fewer than the total of inhabited locations during the height of Israel's nationhood.

Fifteen locations in the tribal region of Benjamin were cited as places where Jews were living during Nehemiah's time. These sites were all north of Jerusalem and were scattered throughout a twenty-seven-mile radius of the city. Some Levites, whose ancestors had lived in Judah at one time, had resettled in Benjamite territory.

- *The remaining Jewish population in the*
- *region lived in thirty-two villages in the*
- *tribal territories of Judah and Benjamin.*
- *Many Levites lived just outside of Jerusalem.*

LISTS OF PRIESTS AND LEVITES (12:1–26)

Nehemiah's concern for the priests and Levites in revitalized Jerusalem was demonstrated with a listing of priests and Levites who had been a part of the original return from Exile almost a century earlier in 538 B.C. He also provided a list of high priests and Levites serving at the time of Joiakim.

Priests and Levites of the First Return (12:1–9)

Twenty-two priestly leaders accompanied Zerubbabel and Jeshua, the first governor and high priest of the resettled country. The twenty-two leaders probably correspond in some way to the twenty-four divisions of priests that David established in preparation for the Jerusalem worship center to be built by Solomon (see 1 Chron. 24:3). Perhaps the smaller number indicates that in 538 B.C. leaders could not be found for two of the divisions.

Zerubbabel served as the first governor of Jerusalem when the Jews returned in 538 B.C. The prophet Haggai referred to him as God's "signet ring," one who possessed God's divine authority and would shape Israelite society for Him (note Hag. 2:23).

Eight different leaders of the nonpriestly Levites that were part of the original return from Exile are also mentioned by Nehemiah. Two of these, Jeshua and Kadmiel, were also mentioned in Ezra's list of returning Levites (see Ezra 2:40). These Levites oversaw the music associated with worship at the Jerusalem Temple, especially the songs of thanksgiving, which were sung antiphonally.

■ *Nehemiah included a list of thirty priests and*
■ *Levites who played a leading role in the Jews'*
■ *return to Jerusalem in 538 B.C.*

High Priests and Levites During the Time of Joiakim (12:10–26)

Nehemiah listed the family line of the high priests that served in Jerusalem since 538 B.C. Six generations are listed. "Jonathan" is probably another name for the priest called Johanan later in this chapter (v. 22).

The names of four heads of priestly families have variant spellings from the list found earlier in the chapter: Shebaniah instead of Shecaniah; Harim instead of Rehum; Meraioth instead of Meremoth; and Miniamin instead of Mijamin.

In addition to the list of individuals that headed priestly families in 538 B.C. (see 12:1–7), Nehemiah included a list of family leaders dating to the days of Joiakim, probably sometime between 520 and 480 B.C. At that time twenty-one of the twenty-two priestly leaders mentioned in the earlier list were still active; Hattush is lacking in the present list.

During the days of Darius the Persian (probably Darius II, who reigned from 423 to 404 B.C.), the Persian government made an official record of the family heads among the Levitical clans as they existed during the period extending through the administrations of four different high priests. The reason for the Persians' interest in this matter is not known; however, it may have been related to taxation issues.

Nehemiah also mentioned six gatekeepers who were in charge of protecting the storerooms at the city gates. The tenure of these individuals was quite lengthy. They administered during the days of the high priest Joiakim, who was active many years prior to Nehemiah's arrival in Jerusalem, as well as during the time period of Nehemiah's leadership.

■ *Nehemiah preserved the names of six gener-*
■ *ations of postexilic high priests, as well as*
■ *the names of key priestly family leaders and*
■ *gatekeepers.*

DEDICATION OF THE WALL (12:27–47)

After the wall surrounding the holy city of Jerusalem was completed, it was formally dedicated to God in a grand celebration that involved festive processions, music, and worship.

Preparations (12:27–30)

For this significant occasion all the Levites living in villages in the tribal territories of Judah and Benjamin were brought to Jerusalem. In keeping with the joyous nature of the event and supported by traditions that went back more than five hundred years to the days of King David (see 1 Chron. 15:16, 19–22; and 25:1–7), the Levites provided both instrumental (cymbals, harps, and lyres) and vocal (antiphonal) music for the occasion.

For the dedication ceremony all the priests and Levites were required to prepare themselves, the general population, the wall, and the gates. This was to be done by bringing all of these into a state of ritual purity, a task accomplished in part by sprinkling these with blood (see Exod. 29:21; Lev. 4:6; 8:11, 30).

■ *Instrumentalists and singers from the tribe of*
■ *Levi, as well as priests and other Jews, all*
■ *purified themselves and came together for a*
■ *special service to dedicate the wall.*

Service of Dedication (12:31–43)

Nehemiah divided the Levitical musicians into two choirs. He directed both choral groups to ascend to the top of the wall and walk in opposite directions toward one another. The first group was led by Ezra and contained leaders from the tribe of Judah, as well as priests with trumpets and Levites with their prescribed musical instruments. They were to walk in a counterclockwise direction, beginning at the southern end of the wall. The second group, equal in size to the first, included Nehemiah and proceeded north in a clockwise direction along the top of the wall.

The two groups met on the northern end of Jerusalem, coming together in a well-coordinated ceremony within the Temple. The governmental officials, priests, and musicians from both groups joined with their counterparts in the worship center. Together the groups joined in hearty singing and festive celebration. The activities were made all the more complete by the participation of women and children in the event. Noise from the celebration could be heard far outside the city limits of Jerusalem. (The mention of noise from the celebration being heard some distance away is like that of the people during the celebration when the Temple's foundation was finished. Note Ezra 3:13.)

■ *Jews marched in two groups on top of the*
■ *wall, meeting at the Temple; there they were*
■ *joined by other Jews for a time of joyous wor-*
■ *ship and celebration.*

Temple Offerings (12:44–47)

A climactic part of the day's events was the formal commissioning of the Levites charged with the responsibility of overseeing the Temple storerooms. Because many Jews had recently promised to bring regular tithes and offerings to the Temple (see Neh. 10:35–39), this commissioning service amounted to a celebration of the people's renewed commitment to God. The tithes were to be used as food for the many individuals associated with the Temple: the priests, the Levites, the musicians, and the gatekeepers. The priests—those who were direct descendants from Aaron, the first high priest—would receive their portion from the Levites' "tithe on the tithe."

During Nehemiah's day the Levites collected the tithe from the cities and towns. A priest, however, would oversee this. Moreover, a tithe on the tithe was brought to the storehouse for the priests in the Temple.

■ *As part of the day's activities, the Jews made*
■ *provision for tithes and offerings to be*
■ *received at the Temple and then distributed*
■ *portions to the priests and Levites serving*
■ *there.*

ADDITIONAL REFORMS (13:1–31)

Nehemiah also was responsible for getting the Jews to make several other reforms in their society. These included the exclusion of non-Jews from their society, restoration of the practice of tithing, enforcement of Sabbath regulations, and halting the practice of marrying non-Jews.

Separation from Foreigners (13:1–3)

On a day of solemn assembly sometime after Nehemiah had returned to Susa to serve in Artaxerxes I's court in 432 B.C., the Jewish community in Jerusalem held a solemn assembly that included a reading from the Law of Moses. Among the passages read was Deuteronomy 23:3–6, a Scripture that forbade all Ammonites and Moabites from ever joining the Israelite assembly. Earlier the Jews had separated themselves from non-Israelites and had pledged not to permit any of their children to marry foreigners (see Neh. 9:2; 10:30). Following the public reading of God's Word, they took the additional step of excluding from their group all who were of non-Israelite descent.

■ *As a result of studying God's Word, the Jews*
■ *decided to exclude all non-Jews from their*
■ *society.*

Tobiah's Expulsion (13:4–9)

This action by the Jewish community created some serious difficulties for Eliashib, the presiding high priest. As the one who controlled the storerooms in Jerusalem's Temple, Eliashib had given Tobiah the Ammonite control of one of the largest of them.

When Nehemiah returned to Jerusalem for a second term as governor there, perhaps sometime around 430 B.C., he was enraged to learn that the high priest had defied God's command and permitted an Ammonite to live on the grounds of the holy Temple. The governor immediately took steps to evict Tobiah, and all of his household goods were thrown out of the Temple area. Then the storeroom was ritually purified and put back into service as a storage facility for the holy utensils, offerings, and incense.

"No Ammonite or Moabite or any of his descendants may enter the assembly of the LORD, even down to the tenth generation" (Deut. 23:3).

■ *Nehemiah had Tobiah the Ammonite's resi-*
■ *dence removed from the Temple grounds and*
■ *the room converted back into space used for*
■ *holy purposes.*

Tithes Restored (13:10–14)

Nehemiah learned that other aspects of the community's religious life had deteriorated as well. Apparently the Jews had reneged on their commitment to bring their tithes and offerings to the Temple. Since the Levites and Levitical singers were not receiving the food they and their families needed to survive, they had to neglect their Temple duties. Nehemiah caused the citizens of the region to renew their giving to the Temple and appointed four trustworthy men—a priest, a scribe, a Levite, and (apparently) a layman—to oversee the distribution of the gifts. Nehemiah was pleased to be able to use his position as governor to help right this wrong, and he asked God to reward him for his efforts.

■ *Nehemiah helped restore the practice of tith-*
■ *ing and took steps to make sure the tithes*
■ *were distributed properly.*

Sabbath Restored (13:15–22)

A further violation of God's Law, and a breach of Israel's contract with Him (see Neh. 10:31), took place in the area of Sabbath regulations. The Jews were performing secular, business-related work on the Sabbath, both in the rural regions surrounding Jerusalem and in the city itself. Nehemiah put an immediate end to these practices by shutting down the Jerusalem marketplace on the Sabbath. He then rebuked both the foreign merchants who conducted business in the city on the Jews' sacred day and the political leaders who had allowed this open breach of God's Law to occur in the first place. Nehemiah's sharpest words were against the Jewish leaders because they knew that God had brought catastrophe on the Israelites in the past when they had violated His commands.

Nehemiah ordered all the gates of Jerusalem to be shut at sundown on Friday, the beginning of the Sabbath, and not to reopen until the Sabbath was over. To enforce his command he stationed some of his own administrative assistants at each gate during the Sabbath. Furthermore, he banned any merchants from conducting business within the immediate vicinity of Jerusalem, threatening to harm them if they violated his order. To guarantee that the Sabbath regulations would not be broken by businessmen in Jerusalem again, Nehemiah assigned the Levites the permanent responsibility of guarding the gates each Sabbath.

■ *Nehemiah took steps to ensure that God's*
■ *Sabbath regulations would be followed*
■ *within the city of Jerusalem.*

Purification from Intermarriage (13:23–31)

Another issue that Nehemiah encountered in his return to Jerusalem was the marriage of Jewish men to women from Ashdod, Ammon, and Moab. These marriages occurred in violation of the Law of Moses (see Deut. 23:3) and the covenant the Jews had made with God during Nehemiah's first term as governor (see Neh. 10:30). Half of the children born into these homes were given so little training regarding the ways of the Jews that they could not even speak Hebrew. Recognizing the severe threat this posed for the spiritual life of the Jews, Nehemiah made a public example of the men who broke this law. He publicly rebuked them, called down curses on them, beat some of them, and then pulled out their hair.

Based on archaeological evidence, the language spoken by post-exilic groups in Ashdod, Ammon, and Moab was Aramaic. It was probably of a dialect different from that spoken by Jews in the Jerusalem area.

Nehemiah was particularly harsh on Joiada, the son of the high priest Eliashib, who had married the daughter of Sanballat, the enemy of the Jews; he was kicked out of Jerusalem. His violation was particularly serious since he was a member of the high priestly line (see Lev. 21:14). Nehemiah compared these men's actions to the sinful marriages King Solomon entered into with foreigners—ones that brought God's judgment on Israel in a former day (see 1 Kings 11:1–13). The governor understood his actions in this matter to be a part of his service to God.

Besides restoring the ritual purity and effectiveness of the priestly and Levitical offices, Nehemiah addressed one final issue related to Temple activity—the problem of inadequate fuel to burn the sacrifices. This problem had come up before during Nehemiah's first term as governor (see Neh. 10:34). Now during his second term, Nehemiah also dealt effectively with this issue. Once again under his leadership, the Jews of the region fulfilled their commitment to provide this essential commodity for God's service.

■ *Nehemiah strictly enforced the prohibition*
■ *against intermarriage with foreign peoples*
■ *and took steps to ensure an adequate fuel*
■ *supply for burning the sacrifices at the Jerus-*
■ *alem Temple.*

QUESTIONS TO GUIDE YOUR STUDY

1. What provisions did Nehemiah make for defending Jerusalem once the wall was built?
2. Describe the revival that God brought through Ezra's leadership.
3. What was the practical result of the revival?
4. Describe the dedication of the wall.

REFERENCE SOURCES USED

The following is a collection of Broadman & Holman published reference sources used for this work. They are provided here to meet the reader's need for more specific information and/or for an expanded treatment of the books of Ezra and Nehemiah. All of these works will greatly aid the reader's study, teaching, and presentation of the books of Ezra and Nehemiah. The accompanying annotations can be helpful in guiding the reader to the proper resources.

Breneman, Mervin. *Ezra, Nehemiah, Esther* (The New American Commentary, vol 10). A scholarly treatment that emphasizes the texts of Ezra and Nehemiah, their backgrounds, theological considerations, issues in interpretation, and summaries of scholarly debates on important points.

Cate, Robert L. *An Introduction to the Historical Books of the Old Testament.* A survey of the books of Joshua through Esther with special attention on issues of history writing in ancient Israel.

Cate, Robert L. *An Introduction to the Old Testament and Its Study.* An introductory work presenting background information, issues related to interpretation, and summaries of each book of the Old Testament.

Dockery, David S., Kenneth A. Mathews, and Robert B. Sloan. *Foundations for Biblical Interpretation: A Complete Library of Tools and Resources.* A comprehensive introduction to matters relating to the composition and interpretation of the entire Bible. This work includes a discussion of the geographical, historical, cultural, religious, and political backgrounds of the Bible.

Farris, T. V. *Mighty to Save: A Study in Old Testament Soteriology.* A wonderful evaluation of many Old Testament passages that teach about salvation. This work makes a conscious attempt to apply Old Testament teachings to the Christian life.

Francisco, Clyde T. *Introducing the Old Testament.* Revised Edition. An introductory guide to each of the books of the Old Testament. This work includes a discussion on how to interpret the Old Testament.

Holman Bible Dictionary. An exhaustive, alphabetically arranged resource of Bible-related subjects. An excellent tool of definitions and other information on people, places, things, and events of the books Ezra and Nehemiah.

Holman Bible Handbook. A summary treatment of each book of the Bible that offers outlines, commentary on key themes and sections, illustrations, charts, maps, and full-color photos. This tool also provides an accent on broader theological teachings of the Bible.

Holman Book of Biblical Charts, Maps, and Reconstructions. This easy-to-use work provides numerous color charts on various matters related to Bible content and background, maps of important events, and drawings of objects, buildings, and cities mentioned in the Bible.

Owens, Mary Frances. *Ezra-Job* (Layman's Bible Book Commentary, vol 7). Contains a concise commentary on Ezra and Nehemiah.

Sandy, D. Brent, and Ronald L. Giese, Jr. *Cracking Old Testament Codes: A Guide to Interpreting the Literary Genres of the Old Testament.* This book is designed to make scholarly discussions available to preachers and teachers.

Smith, Ralph L. *Old Testament Theology: Its History, Method, and Message.* A comprehensive treatment of various issues relating to Old Testament theology. Written for university and seminary students, ministers, and advanced lay teachers.

SHEPHERD'S
NOTES

SHEPHERD'S
NOTES